A Cultural History of Japanese Women's Language

Michigan Monograph Series in Japanese Studies
Number 57

Center for Japanese Studies
The University of Michigan

A Cultural History of Japanese Women's Language

Endō Orie

Center for Japanese Studies
The University of Michigan
Ann Arbor   2006

Published by the Center for Japanese Studies,
The University of Michigan
1007 E. Huron St.
Ann Arbor, MI 48104-1690

Library of Congress Cataloging in Publication Data

Endo, Orie, 1938–
    [Onna no kotoba no bunkashi. English]
    A Cultural history of Japanese women's language / Endo Orie.
        p. cm. — (Michigan monograph series in Japanese studies ; no. 57)
    Includes bibliographical references and index.
    ISBN 1-929280-39-4 (cloth : alk. paper)
    1. Japanese language—Sex differences. 2. Women—Japan—Language.
I. Title.

PL698.W65E5313 2006
495.6082—dc22

2006049251

This book was set in Palatino Macron.

This publication meets the ANSI/NISO Standards for Permanence of Paper
for Publications and Documents in Libraries and Archives (Z39.48—1992).

Printed in the United States of America

CONTENTS

LIST OF TABLES

PREFACE

In October 1993, with the support of Ms. Suzuki Kazuki in the editorial department of *Japan Quarterly*, I published a short essay titled "Sexism in Japanese-Language Dictionaries." Almost as soon as the article appeared in print, a publisher in England suggested that I write a book on the same theme. Ultimately, that particular proposal never came to fruition, but my own ambition to clarify the nature of Japanese discriminatory language for non-Japanese readers grew stronger. First of all, I wanted students of the Japanese language who were studying abroad to realize that women didn't necessarily use the so-called the "feminine" language presented in Japanese language textbooks; and, second, I wanted to convey to readers that the sexist language in Japanese, far from an essential and natural aspect of Japanese, was in fact constructed by a specific social-historical system.

I spent the next four years in and out of libraries researching the cultural history of "women's language" from ancient times to the present. The book that resulted from these efforts was first published as *Onna no kotoba no bunka-shi* (A Cultural History of Women's Language) by Gakuyō shobō. To my great pleasure, not only was the book well received by readers with an interest in the topic, but it was used as a text for university courses and community education programs.

Encouraged by this interest in the book, I returned to the idea of publishing an English version. With the support of a translation grant from the Japanese Ministry of Education, I was able to arrange for a translation of the original Japanese through the combined efforts of Geraldine Harcourt and Heather Souter and for editorial revisions by Claire Marie. To each of these three talented translators and scholars, I owe a great debt of gratitude. The editorial staff at the Center for Japanese Studies Publications at the University of Michigan—Bruce Willoughby, Robert Mory, and Leslie Pincus—went over the manuscript with a fine-tooth comb and a sharp eye. Thanks to their generosity and professional discernment, this long-awaited English-language edition of *A Cultural History of Japanese Women's Language* has finally reached print. It is especially gratifying to present this book to my husband, Endō Akira, just a few months after he received the Japan Prize for his discovery of Statin, a pharmaceutical cure for high cholesterol.

INTRODUCTION

According to figures compiled by the Japan Foundation (2003), over 2,350,000 non-Japanese are currently studying Japanese or conducting research on the Japanese language. The figure increases when one includes those who are merely interested in Japan. A recent edition of *Mainichi Shinbun*, a national newspaper, reported on French enthusiasm for the Japanese language: "Due to the popularity of Pokemon and Pikachū, the number of children [in France] learning Japanese in order to understand Japanese comic books is rapidly increasing" (Evening edition, April 15, 2000). Regardless of the reason for the boom, or how deeply it runs, as a Japanese person I am delighted at the increase in the number of people with some connection to the Japanese language, and I hope that these people accurately learn about the Japanese language, particularly the language of women.

People interested in Japanese and students of the language first refer to introductory outlines in general textbooks. Students usually trust whatever is written in those textbooks, but should they? Let us briefly consider the content of these texts. In general, they begin with explanations of the sound system, grammar, lexicon, and orthography of Japanese, almost always followed by comments about gender differences predominant in the language. For example, "[Japanese] is divided into women's language and men's language according to the language user's sex" (Katō 1989, 2). Similarly, "a characteristic of the Japanese language is that men and women use different expressions" (Tamamura 1995, 3). As a woman who uses Japanese everyday, as a Japanese language educator, and as a Japanese language researcher, I find myself questioning these statements. First, what is "women's language"? Is the language I use "women's language" merely because I am a woman? Personally, I do not believe that my usage differs substantially from that of men, so does this mean that I speak something other than "women's language"?

The textbooks cited above do not provide definitions for "men's language" or "women's language"—in fact, definitions for "women's language," "men's language," or "women's speech style" are difficult to find anywhere. Let us look at the definition provided by *Kōjien* (5th ed.), a typical Japanese language dictionary.

1

Joseigo (women's language): a style of expression unique to women, manifested in lexicon, style, and pronunciation. Marked by the avoidance of *kango* terms (i.e., terms of Chinese origin) in the Heian period, it is particularly prominent from the Muromachi period onwards in the language of the female attendants to the imperial court (*nyōbō-kotoba*) and the language of courtesans (*yūjogo*). Also marked by the use of the honorific prefix *o*, sentence-final particles *yo*, *wa*, interjections *sa*, *ne*, and in other aspects of the lexicon and pronunciation in contemporary language. It is also known as *fujingo* "ladies' language."

It is important to note that *Kōjien* does not provide an entry for *danseigo*, "men's language."

The dictionary entry quoted above does not satisfy my doubts about "women's language." In fact, it raises new questions. Is this "style of expression unique to women" actually used only by women? Can we call both *nyōbō-kotoba*, the style used by attendants to the imperial court in the medieval era, and *yūjogo*, the style used by courtesans and prostitutes in the Edo period, "women's language"? Are the honorific prefix *o*, sentence-final particles *yo* and *wa*, and interjections *sa* and *ne* peculiar only to women in contemporary Japanese? Furthermore, the dictionary entry gives us no indication as to whether "women's language" and "men's language" are as prominent a characteristic of the Japanese language as the textbook outlines suggest.

According to dictionary entries such as the one quoted above, contemporary "women's language" does not refer to women's usage in general, but to specific words. Is it appropriate to label one small subset of the language, such as *o* and *yo*, as "women's language" merely because women use these expressions? Furthermore—and this is the point that I find most fundamentally problematic—is it really only women who use the honorific prefix *o* and sentence-final particle *yo*? I certainly do not feel that the language I and other women use differs greatly from that of men.

It would indeed be unfortunate for the language if superficial interest was focused on Japanese because it supposedly has a "women's language" that was "unique" and "exotic," or again, if observers draw hasty conclusions about Japanese being different from "our" (i.e., other) languages. I do not deny that words unique to women's usage exist in Japanese, and the speech of women of my mother's generation differs from language used by men. We need, however, to grasp the relationship between Japanese and the women who use it within Japan's socio-historical context. Have words used exclusively by women existed since the beginning of the Japanese language? How is language used at present? If we consider these issues within historical contexts, we can avoid the kind of one-sided explanations seen in grammar overviews that emphasize gender differences and declare them to be a defining characteristic of the Japanese language.

In the following chapters, I aim to convey to readers how historical processes have shaped the language of women in Japan and to place the current state of the Japanese language in historical perspective. Taking this approach, we see gender differences in usage arising where none existed before, largely due to social and political factors, and then gradually disappearing due to a different set of social and political factors.

In chapter 1, I look at the literature of the Nara (710–94) and Heian (794–1192) periods in search of gender differences in usage. Do the male and female characters in the *Kojiki*, a compilation of mythology and early history written in 712, speak in gender-marked styles? Are there differences between the poetic diction of male and that of female poets in the *Man'yōshū*, the first extant anthology of poetry, and its Heian period successors, such as the *Kokinshū*? I also look at the effects of the custom of teaching only males to read and write *kanji* "Chinese characters."

In chapter 2, I describe the political, social, and religious changes that swept over Japan beginning in the 12th century, particularly as they affected the culture's view of women and the standards of behavior expected of women and girls. I also look at *nyōbō-kotoba*, the language of imperial court attendants in the 14th and 15th centuries, as an extreme outcome of these new attitudes.

In chapter 3, I show how the spread of Confucian philosophy during the 17th and 18th centuries further decreased the status of women, and I look at the way in which Confucian principles were applied to the education of young girls. I also describe *yūjogo*, the language used by the prostitutes during that period.

In chapter 4, I explain how the development of a national educational system during the Meiji period (1868–1912) spread so-called "feminine" language to women of all social classes.

In chapter 5, I trace the development of women's language through the social and political changes of the Shōwa period (1926–89). I show how the language of both men and women changed in response to urbanization, war, and foreign influences.

In chapter 6, I look at the language of contemporary women with a focus on *ryūkōgo* "current slang and colloquialisms." The current social environment, in which young women are free as never before to define their own identities, has had noteworthy effects on women's use of language.

We will commence our exploration of the relationship between women and the Japanese language by examining a variety of classical texts,

3

beginning with those from ancient times and looking in turn at sources from the medieval, premodern, modern, and contemporary periods. Doing so will illuminate the centuries-long ambivalent relationship between women and the Japanese language. We also will be able to answer many of the questions we have about the relationship between gender and the Japanese language and will inevitably be left with others to ponder.

CHAPTER 1
WOMEN AND THE ANCIENT LANGUAGE

In this chapter, I shall outline the relationship between women and the Japanese language from early historic times to the end of the Heian period (794–1192). Since there are almost no contemporary records of actual spoken language, the discussion will be limited to what surviving documents and literary texts can tell us. In particular, I shall focus on the part that women played in the formation of the Japanese writing system and the production of literature, as well as on their position in society.

WOMEN'S LANGUAGE IN THE *KOJIKI* AND THE *MAN'YŌSHŪ*

Japan's oldest extant chronicle, the *Kojiki* (Record of Ancient Matters) was completed during the Nara period (710–94) in 712. Compiled by Ō no Yasumaro, it is said to be a transcription of myths that had been memorized by the female court attendant Hieda no Are.

It contains an exchange between the god Izanagi no Mikoto and the goddess Izanami no Mikoto, who together gave birth to the land of Japan. Having been entrusted with this task, the two deities perform a marriage rite by walking in a circle around a heavenly pillar, the male from the left and the female from the right, until they meet. At the sight of Izanagi, Izanami speaks first, saying *Ana-ni-yashi e wotoko wo*, "How good a man!" to which Izanagi then responds *Ana-ni-yashi e wotome wo*, "How good a woman!" The offspring of their union, however, is not a perfectly formed island, which Izanagi attributes to the fact that Izanami spoke first. They therefore repeat the ritual. This time the male speaks first and the female responds to his words; and this time, according to the legend, the products of their union are the splendidly formed islands that make up present-day Japan.

This account has two features of interest to us. The first is the complete lack of differentiation between the woman's words, *Ana-ni-yashi e wotoko wo*, and the man's, *Ana-ni-yashi e wotome wo*; the sole point of difference is the nouns, *wotoko* "man" and *wotome* "woman." The second is the significance of the woman speaking first. Since Izanagi no Mikoto blames this for their initial failure, and since they succeed in bearing a perfectly formed island when the order is reversed, the story attests to a male preoccupation with dominance.

Yet it is important to note that the woman indeed speaks first. In his 1920 book on women's issues in Japanese literature the writer Shirayanagi Shūko (1884–1954) remarks on this fact: "We must also consider the possibility that women were so powerful that the rule that it was not proper for a woman to speak before a man had to be established in order to prevent women from outdoing men" (Shirayanagi 1920, 66).

The two deities may well have alternated in dominance, with the husband taking the initiative at times and the wife at others. This exchange, which is found in a myth of national origins, tells us that speaking first was not always the man's prerogative, nor was it always the woman's. As far as we can determine from this conversation and others in the 8th-century *Kojiki*, there is no gender differentiation in the language, and the gods and goddesses are equally dominant.

Now let us turn to the question of gendered language in the earliest extant collection of Japanese poetry, the *Man'yōshū* (Collection of Ten Thousand Leaves), which is believed to have been completed in about 759 A.D. Compiled by the poet Ōtomo no Yakamochi (716–85), the anthology contains poems composed by some 530 people (Hisamatsu 1962, 947), both men and women, from a variety of social classes: emperors, priests, officials, soldiers stationed in Kyūshū, and even beggars. There are approximately 4,500 works of two types: *tanka* "short poems" (referred to hereafter as *waka* "Japanese poems"), which consist of thirty-one syllables in the pattern 5-7-5-7-7, and *chōka* "long poems," which consist of any number of alternating 5- and 7-syllable lines. No gender differences can be seen in either type. For example, there is no way to tell which of these two verses is written by a man and which by a woman.

> *Nigita-zu ni funanori sen to tsuki mateba*
> *shio mo kanahinu ima wa kogiide na*

> We have waited for the moon to board ship at Nigita harbor, and with the moonrise the tides too are right. Now let us set out.

> *Shirogane mo kogane mo tama mo nani semu ni*
> *masareru takara ko ni shikame ya mo*

> What worth is there in silver or gold or jewels? For there is indeed no treasure greater than a child.

The former is the work of a woman, Nukata no Ōkimi, and the latter that of a man, Yamanoe no Okura, although it is extremely difficult to guess this fact simply by looking at their poems.

Some Japanese language scholars have studied the influence of gender in *waka* by examining the occurrence of certain vocabulary. Saeki Umetomo (1936, 91) investigates the use of the second person singular *kimi* in the *Man'yōshū*. He reports that it is used only by women addressing men and not vice versa, a conclusion which he bases on an editorial annotation to poem No. 3,261 in book 13, in which a male poet uses *kimi*. The poem has been annotated *Ri ni awazu* "against reason." While I am neither a *Man'yōshū* scholar nor an expert on *tanka* or *waka*, I cannot go along with Saeki's conclusion. The poet did write *kimi*, and if one looks objectively, not at the vague annotation, but at the actual word, it certainly qualifies as an example of male use, even though it may be a rare one.[1]

Another Japanese language scholar, Hamada Atsushi (1946, 107), states that *kimi* is "a word used very frequently, particularly in the *Kojiki*, *Nihonshoki* (Chronicles of Japan), and *Man'yōshū*," but he makes no mention of a gender difference. Even if we accept Saeki's conclusion that the use of *kimi* was gender-bound, this may apply only to its use in *tanka* or *waka*. We know nothing about gender differences in other spheres of usage.

At least as late as the period represented in the *Man'yōshū*, it appears that there were no clearly defined gender differences in linguistic usage. Mashimo Saburō (1948, 20) says of the Nara period that "it remains doubtful whether there were distinctions between men's and women's speech in general conversation. The differences, if any, were very slight, and thus neither men nor women would have experienced a strong sense of differentiation."

GENDER DIFFERENCES IN THE LANGUAGE OF THE HEIAN PERIOD

Early Heian period literature and historical records make no reference to gender differences in language. However, one mid-Heian period text is often cited as an explicit reference. This is section 4 (6 in Ivan Morris's translation) of the *Makura no sōshi* (The Pillow Book) a collection of occasional writings by the court lady Sei Shōnagon, completed in about 1017. In the version published by Shōgakkan, which I refer to hereafter as "the Shōgakkan text,"[2] the passage reads:

> *Koto kotonaru mono, hōshi no kotoba, otoko omina no kotoba.*
> *Gesu no kotoba ni wa kanarazu moji amashitari.* (20)

> Different Ways of Speaking
> A priest's language.
> The speech of men and of women.

7

The common people always tend to add extra syllables to their
words. (Morris 1967, 27)

Many people consider this passage to be recognition of gender differences in
the language of Sei Shōnagon's time, taking it to mean that priests and laity,
men and women, and commoners and the nobility all spoke in contrasting
styles.

Over the course of nine centuries, however, the *Makura no sōshi* has
been handed down in a number of versions that are consistent in their broad
outlines but vary in their minute details, due to misreading and mistakes
in the hand copying of manuscripts. In one of these variant editions, the
Gunsho ruijubon, the passage appears as follows:

> *Onaji koto naredo. Kikimimi koto naru mono. Hōshi no kotoba.*
> *Otoko no kotoba. Yoki hito no kotoba. Gesu no kotoba….*

> Cases in which people say the same thing but sound different:
> A priest's speech.
> The speech of men.
> The speech of a noble person.
> The speech of the common people….

The Shōgakkan text's "speech of men and women" appears here as "speech
of men," and there is an added mention of nobility. Mozume Takakazu
(1922, 6) interprets this version as meaning that the speech of priests "sounds
different from that of Sei Shōnagon herself, who is a member of the laity,"
while men's speech is perceived as different "when heard from the viewpoint
of a woman." According to Mozume's reading, Sei Shōnagon is giving her
impression that men's speech sounds different from women's in terms of
pitch, volume, and stress, not at the level of vocabulary or grammar.

Even if the Shōgakkan text quoted above is a true representation
of Sei Shōnagon's intentions, Kunida Yuriko (1964, 2) advises caution in
concluding from this one passage that gender differences existed in the
language of the Heian period. "It is possible to interpret Sei Shōnagon's
comment … on differences in the language of men, women, and priests to
mean that women's language already existed by the middle of the Heian
period, but since the differences are not described anywhere, even in *Makura
no sōshi*, it is in fact difficult to believe that women's language was established
in a distinct and clear-cut form."

By the early 11th century, when Sei Shōnagon was compiling her
Makura no sōshi, numerous *monogatari*, "tales," had been written, and the
diary genre was also flourishing. The writer Murasaki Shikibu had already

completed her 54-volume *Genji monogatari* (The Tale of Genji), famed as the world's oldest novel, in 1008. None of the extant works, however, contains any reference to differentiation of language by gender. Mashimo Saburō explains that "women's language in this period differed from men's in only a very few respects" (1948, 20).

Let us look at an actual conversation between a man and a woman in *Genji*.[3] This exchange takes place in the volume "Evening Mist" between Kumoinokari, a woman, and Yūgiri, her husband. It is not an everyday conversation, being part of a scene in which Kumoinokari rebukes her husband for his inconstancy; it is clear, however, that she is using rougher speech, while he employs polite language containing many honorific expressions, a reversal of the usual stereotype.

> Kumoinokari: *Nanigoto ifu zo to yo. Oiraka ni shini-tamahine. Maromo shinamu. Mireba nikushi. Kikeba aikyo nashi.*
>
> That will do. Just die, please, if you do not mind, and I will hurry and do the same. I hate the sight of you and I do not like the sound of you....
>
> Man: *Chikakute koso wa mi-tamahazarame. Yoso ni wa nanika kiki-tamahazaramu. Sate mo chigiri fukakanaru se wo shirasemu no mikokoro nari.*
>
> Oh, but you would still hear about me. How do you propose to avoid that unpleasantness? Are you trying to tell me that there is a strong bond between us?

Here is an example of an ordinary conversation, from the "Morning Glory" chapter between Prince Genji and his protégée, and later mistress, Murasaki.

> Prince Genji: *Ayashiku keshiki no kawareru beki koro ka na.... Midatenaku obosaruru ni ya to taeoku wo mata ikaga.*
>
> "You seem so touchy these days.... I have not wanted to be taken for granted, like a familiar and rumpled old robe, and so I have been staying away a little more than I used to."
>
> Murasaki: *Nareyuku koso geni uki koto ohokare.*
>
> "Yes, it is true. One does not enjoy being taken for granted."

This conversation contains no honorifics and no discernible gender differences. While there are many differences due to social status in the way

9

the characters speak in *Genji monogatari*, these are not gender-related. It is very difficult to ascertain how women of the common classes spoke during this period. There are no works written by these women that remain, and very few literary works make reference to them. One such example is the expressions that Sei Shōnagon finds as vulgar in her work *Makura no sōshi*. The following is an extract from the women's rice-planting poem in section 248.

> *Kakku yo, ore yo. Kayatsu yo. Ore nakitezo, ware wa ta ni tatsu.*
>
> Oh little cuckoo. Oh, cuckoo. You, there. I am in this field because you call.

Another such example is from *Konjaku monogatari*. In section 18 [28], the lewd Matsutano Shigekata is recalling how he once again fell into his wife's trap. The following quotes of his wife's speech contain orders, declarations, and derogatory expressions such as *onore* (you swine), *yuke* (go), *sha ashi uchiworitemu* ([I'll] break your legs), *anakama* (lit., noisy, "shut up"), and *kono shiremono* (fool).

> *Onore wa sono kesaushitsuru onna no moto ni ike. Ware ga moto ni kitari tewa, kanarazu sha ashi uchiworitemu mono zo.*
>
> "You swine, go to the girl you've fallen for. If you come near me I'll break your legs."
>
> *Anakama, kono shiremono. Meshihi no yau ni hito no keshiki wo mo emishirazu, koe wo mo ekikishirade, soko wo sagashite hito ni waraharuru wa, imijiki shirekoto ni wa arazu ya.*
>
> "Shut up you fool. As if a blind man you can't sense your own wife's feelings, showing your stupidity at not being able to tell her voice, you are a laughing stock, I am amazed at you."

WOMEN AND LITERATURE IN THE NARA AND HEIAN PERIODS

Before examining the relationship of women to the development of literary language, I would like briefly to assess the extent of women's contributions to literature during the eras of the Nara and Heian courts.

The *Man'yōshū* includes poems by 106 women, ranging from empresses to wives of the soldiers in the Kyūshū garrison. This number represents 20 percent of the total of 530 contributors. After the *Man'yōshū*, a total of twenty-one poetry anthologies were commissioned by an emperor or retired emperor, from the 10th-century *Kokinshū* to the 15th-century *Shin zoku kokinshū*. From 130 to 914 poets are represented in each of these imperial anthologies, with women accounting for a maximum of 90 and a minimum of 4.

From the *Kokinshū*, which was completed about 914, to the *Kin'yōshū*, completed about 1127, women made up at least 20 percent and sometimes as much as 30 percent of the contributors. With the *Shikashū* (ca. 1151), however, their numbers fall below 10 percent, and their numbers remain low until the series ends with the *Shin zoku kokinshū* (ca. 1446).

Thus, between the eras of the *Man'yōshū* and the *Kin'yōshū*—the 8th to the early 12th century—the creative activity of women poets flourished to an extent that is quite comparable with that of male poets. Furthermore, the twenty volumes of the *Man'yōshū* are believed to have been compiled by various hands, and there are indications that a woman was involved. While the central editorial role has been attributed with certainty to the poet Ōtomo no Yakamochi, some volumes are thought to have been partially or even completely the work of other people, including Ōtomo no Sakanoue no Iratsume, the matriarch of the Ōtomo clan, who was both the aunt and mother-in-law of Yakamochi.

Gotō Toshio (1986, 25) and Itami Sueo (1988, 68) are among those who believe that Lady Ōtomo was the compiler of volumes 3, 4, 6, and 8. They cite such evidence as the fact that all of these volumes contain poems by Lady Ōtomo. In addition, the annotations of her poems take a viewpoint beyond that expected of a poet or a contributor of material, and the notes on her career are excessively detailed, providing information that only she could have known.

That a woman could have played a part in compiling Japan's oldest and best-known poetry anthology points to the strength of women's position in the literary world of this period and to the vigor of their activity.

Having looked at the situation in the world of verse, I shall survey women's contribution to prose literature by comparing the percentage of works by women writers in each age. I have based my comparison on a chronology of literary history produced by one of Japan's most prominent publishing companies. I have counted all the listed works of known authorship and also those which are attributed to an author of known gender, classifying the number of works according to gender and period as shown in table 1, using intervals of 100 years from the 8th to the 19th century and fifty years from 1900 onward.

Table 1. Comparison of numbers of literary works, by gender of author

	Male	Female
710-799	5	0
800-899	3	0
900-999	12	1
1000-1099	1	10
1100-1199	7	1
1200-1299	19	3
1300-1399	10	1
1400-1499	7	0
1500-1599	0	0
1600-1699	17	0
1700-1799	23	0
1800-1899	50	2
1900-1949	98	6
1950-1988	60	12

Source: "Chronology of Literary History," in *Nihongo Daijiten* (Unabridged Japanese Dictionary) (Kōdansha, 1989).

As can be seen in the table, works by women writers appear between the tenth and fourteenth centuries, and again from the 19th century onward.[4] During the time from the 15th century to the 18th century, no works by women appeared.

WOMEN AND THE DEVELOPMENT OF *HIRAGANA*

Great changes took place in the written form of the Japanese language during the Nara and Heian periods. Among the causes of these changes were the particular needs of women with respect to the written word; and women's literary activity was, in turn, greatly influenced by the results of the changes. This new phase in the writing of Japanese began with the compilation of the *Man'yōshū*.

The Japanese had not developed an indigenous script when they borrowed the Chinese characters or *kanjj* that reached their islands via the Korean Peninsula in about the 3rd or 4th century. Initially, the texts written in *kanji* were actually composed in classical Chinese, or *kanbun*. That is, in order to commit the Japanese vernacular to writing, one first translated it into Chinese and wrote it down in *kanji*. In this bilingual system, government officials, priests, and scholars learned and employed written Chinese.

Gradually, however, many inconsistencies emerged. For one thing, the system could not easily accommodate indigenous Japanese geographical and personal names essential for record keeping. Moreover, since not all users were equally proficient, some mixed Japanese-style grammar into their Chinese, despite the fact that the two languages are structurally very different. Some even introduced inflected verbs, case particles such as *ga*, *wa*, and *ni*, and auxiliary verbs—all of which exist in Japanese but not in Chinese—into their Chinese prose.

Out of this confusion arose a method of representing indigenous Japanese words by using Chinese characters for their pronunciation only, not for their meaning. From there, the next step was to represent all elements of the Japanese language using only the pronunciation of the *kanji*. Since this set of unmodified Chinese characters was used in the poems of the *Man'yōshū* they were called *man'yōgana* (from *kana* "script").

Man'yōgana made it possible to represent texts in the Japanese language without having first to translate them into Chinese. The *kanji* served as phonetic symbols regardless of their own original meaning.

The standard way of writing Chinese characters at the time was the square style known as *kaisho*, with straight lines and angular strokes contained in a square frame. As *man'yōgana* came into wider use, and as the characters were written hastily or carelessly, they were gradually simplified and changed into a more cursive form, which spread rapidly, due to its speed and simplicity. Meanwhile, the officials, priests, and scholars sought to maintain their prestige and their distance from the common people by insisting that the only proper way to represent Japanese was in *kanbun* with Chinese characters, which they used for all government documents and notices, historical records, Buddhist scriptures, and other official texts.

Verse literature also fell into two distinct genres: the *tanka* "short song" or *waka* "Japanese song" indigenous to Japan and found in the *Man'yōshū*, and the *kanshi* "Chinese poem," which was introduced from China. *Waka* were produced by people in every station of life, from emperors, empresses, and government officials to beggars. *Kanshi*, however, were produced only by males of high status, including emperors, high priests, and scholars. In the society of this period, *kanshi* and *kanbun* were the official, public forms of expression used ceremonially, while *waka* and prose written in Japanese were the personal, private forms for everyday life.

Man'yōgana became progressively simpler in form during the Heian period, as people began writing in a more cursive style, which eventually gave rise to *hiragana*, the phonetic syllabary that is used today. In *man'yōgana*, any one of a number of characters with the same pronunciation could be used, according to the writer's preference, to represent the same sound. This confusing use of multiple characters for a single sound gradually gave way to a unified system of *hiragana* in which there is supposed to be one symbol for each sound. The Japanese language could thereafter be written entirely in *hiragana*, which gave the Japanese a script of their own.

There are alternative theories which attribute the creation of *hiragana* to men and to women, but the former currently has wider support among scholars of the Japanese language (Hayashi 1988, 77). The claim of male authorship is based on the fact that a simplified script approaching the present form of *hiragana* has been discovered on the back of Buddhist statues in old temples and among the *man'yōgana* of official requests for promotion written by provincial governors, and in both cases the authors of such texts are known to have been male. Because there are no similarly documented cases of proven female authorship, it is claimed that women did not contribute to the creation of *hiragana*.

One advocate of a theory of female authorship is Yoshizawa Yoshinori (1934, 29–35). His argument can be summarized as follows: In the society of the time, women did not have the opportunity to receive instruction in reading and writing Chinese characters. Yet the exchange of *waka* during love affairs was a custom of great importance to aristocratic women, and unlike men, who already had access to Chinese characters, they needed a script of their own.

Yoshizawa's contention that women were unable to receive instruction in Chinese characters calls for closer examination. It is known that certain women in the Nara and Heian periods had an advanced knowledge of both Chinese characters and k*anbun*. In the Nara period, women who were exceptionally talented at writing were engaged as *nyokan* "minor court ladies" and charged with preparation of official documents written in *kanbun*.

An emperor's daughter composed excellent Chinese poetry at the age of seventeen and was awarded the rank of *sanbon* (third rank in the imperial family) by her father.[5] Murasaki Shikibu gave the Second Empress, at her own request, instruction in the Chinese book *Yue Fū*. The passage in *Makura no sōshi* [193/188] which reads "Writings In Chinese. The collected works of Po Chū-i. The Anthology. Requests for promotion written by Doctors of Literature" (Morris 1967, 188) suggests that Sei Shōnagon must have been well-versed in the Chinese classics to be able to single out for praise the two volumes she names here.[6]

Thus, In the Nara period and the early Heian period (i.e., until the 9th century), talented women who found themselves in a favorable environment could enjoy the benefits of education in Chinese characters and *kanbun*. From about the beginning of the 10th century, however, such familiarity with Chinese writing came to be frowned on and regarded as unfeminine.

Yoshizawa cites two passages that are indicative of the difference between men's and women's education in the 11th century. As evidence that Chinese characters and *kanbun* were not considered part of a girl's education, he quotes section 20 [22] of *Makura no sōshi*, in which Koichijō Sadaijin, the Minister of the Left who lived in the Smaller Palace of the First Ward, is reported to have given his daughter this advice: "First you must study penmanship. Next you must learn to play the seven-string zither better than anyone else. And also you must memorize all the poems in the twenty volumes of the *Kokinshū*" (Morris 1967, 18).

On male education, he quotes a *kanbun* passage from *Kujōdono ikai* (The Admonitions to Posterity of Lord Kujō), by Fujiwara no Morosuke (908–60), which prescribes Chinese studies as the first requirement for boys: "When a boy grows old enough to understand, have him first learn the Chinese classics, then calligraphy, and then music and dance." In view of the clear distinction that these writers make between boys' and girls' education, Yoshizawa concludes that girls had no opportunity to learn Chinese characters.

References to differences between male and female education can also be found in *Genji*. In the first volume, "The Paulownia Court," the brilliance of the young Prince Genji is illustrated by this statement: "When he was seven he went through the ceremonial reading of the Chinese classics, and never before had there been so fine a performance" (Seidensticker, p. 13). This reference suggests that a boy's commencement of the study of the Chinese classics at the age of seven was marked by a special ceremony.

In the fifth volume, "Lavender," there is a description of the early education that Prince Genji gives Murasaki the heroine of the tale, who at that time is called Waka Murasaki "Young Murasaki." Waka Murasaki is taken in as a young child by Prince Genji, having lost her mother and the grandmother who was looking after her. Genji instructs her personally in various subjects with the intention of raising her as an ideal woman. First, he makes samples of writing and pictures for her to copy. Next, he composes a *waka* and has her copy it with the brush. When the girl hesitates and says she can't, Genji tells her that even if she cannot write well, she must practice.

Volume 8, "The Festival of the Cherry Blossoms," contains a reference to teaching Waka Murasaki the *koto*. In volume 10, "The Sacred Tree," there is a scene in which Prince Genji is satisfied that Waka Murasaki's writing of *kana* has improved, and congratulates himself on having raised her as he had intended. Among all these references to the girl's education, there is no

15

mention of teaching her Chinese characters or the Chinese classics.

Furthermore, Murasaki Shikibu says in her diary that when her younger brother (later to become Secretary in the Ministry of Ceremonies) was studying the Chinese classics as a child, she always sat nearby, listening and learning as he read aloud. Her brother was a slow learner and often forgot the readings, but she mastered them with such remarkable speed that their father, who prized learning, lamented that she was not born a boy.

These references in tales and diaries seem to bear out Yoshizawa's view that—except in special cases—boys were generally taught Chinese characters and the classics, while girls were not given the opportunity to receive such an education. Yoshizawa also cites several instances that indicate that aristocratic Heian society disapproved of women having contact with Chinese characters and books.

First, in section 86 [78] of *Makura no sōshi*, Sei Shōnagon is asked to complete a stanza of a Chinese poem. Although she does in fact know the poem and could have completed the verse in the Chinese style, she notes that "I had to prove that I knew the next line of the poem, but were I to write it in my somewhat faltering Chinese characters it would make a bad impression" (Morris 1967, 72).[7] She therefore uses the kana script to complete the stanza with part of a Japanese poem on the same theme. In other words, although Sei Shōnagon knows her Chinese poetry and is sure of the characters, she deliberately deprecates and conceals her skill because she does not want to be seen as a "know-it-all."

Yoshizawa also introduces a passage from *Murasaki shikibu nikki* (The Diary of Murasaki Shikibu) which tells how Murasaki takes out her late husband's Chinese books to while away the time and hears her ladies-in-waiting talking. One says: "It's because the mistress is always so familiar with Chinese books and the like that she has such ill luck. Why would a lady read books in *kanbun*? In the old days, it wasn't done even to read the sutras." Apparently there was a superstitious belief that a woman being familiar with the Chinese classics would bring misfortune.

There are many similar episodes, not quoted by Yoshizawa, which indicate that a woman's interest in Chinese characters and the Chinese classics was not socially acceptable. In the second volume of *Genji*, "The Broom Tree," there is a scene, known as "Comparisons on a Rainy Night," in which several young men regale one another with stories of the women they have known. The young man from the Ministry of Ceremonies tells an exaggerated tale of how, when he had an affair with the daughter of a learned scholar, he was put off by the way she spoke using a great many Chinese words. He gives an example: "I have been indisposed with a malady known as coryza. Discommoded to an uncommon degree. I have been imbibing of a steeped potion made from bulbaceous herbs. Because of the noisome odor, I will not find it possible to admit of greater propinquity" (Seidensticker, p. 36). Where the words *kaze, netsu, kusuri, nomu,* and *ome ni kakaru* ("cold," "fever," "medicine," "drink," and "meet,") would suffice, he says she used the sinicized *fubyō, gokunechi, sōyaku, fukusu,* and *taimen* (which Seidensticker renders in fancy Latinate terms). She is the butt of ridicule among the men, who find a young woman's use of Chinese expressions decidedly unattractive.

Later in the same scene, the officer comments: "The very worst are the ones who scribble off Chinese characters at such a rate that they fill a good half of letters where they are most out of place, letters to other women. 'What a bore,' you say. 'If only she had mastered a few of the feminine things'" (Seidensticker, p. 36). Clearly, Murasaki's male contemporaries considered it unfeminine and inappropriate for women to write in Chinese characters.

To take one last example from *Genji*: in volume 21, "The Maiden," there is a scene in which Genji, the professors, and several courtiers compose Chinese poems together. The author describes how the participants are assigned to write their poems according to different rules or styles; she notes that they "brought in numerous old precedents," and says that all of the poems are interesting. Then she concludes, "But it would not be seemly for a woman to speak in detail of these scholarly happenings, and I shall say no more" (Seidensticker, p. 363). Having already made a number of well-informed remarks on Chinese poetry, Murasaki evidently felt obliged to add this disclaimer—a clear indication of the prevailing bias. Given this social climate, it is easy to understand the circumstances in which women looked to *hiragana* as their medium of expression.

The calligrapher Komai Gasei (1951) is another proponent of women as the originators of *hiragana*. He writes: "Because [women in the Heian period], unlike those of the Nara Period, were excluded from an education in Chinese studies, they wrote *man'yōgana* with no knowledge of Chinese characters. Whereas men, knowing the meanings of the characters, might have hesitated to string them together phonetically, women could do this without inhibition because, being women, they did not know their literal meanings, and furthermore, they could freely alter and simplify the forms of characters. Thus complex elements were removed, the change was made to a simple method of transcription, and the script came to be written more beautifully, guided by the innately graceful feminine aesthetic sense. The result was *hiragana*" (Komai 1951, 53).

If women's ignorance of Chinese characters was a blessing in disguise, as Komai suggests, then it was surely a mixed one, and his stereotypical attribution of an "innately graceful feminine aesthetic sense" is equally problematic. Nevertheless there is something persuasive about Komai's crediting the undoubted beauty of the resulting script to the fact that women were free to simplify Chinese characters unrestricted by their meanings.

More than three hundred years elapsed between the development of *man'yōgana* and the establishment of the *hiragana* syllabary in its final form. Over these centuries, the script evolved from an initial modified style that was very close to *kaisho*, gradually becoming more cursive until it arrived at the fluid softness of *hiragana*, which retains no trace of *kaisho's* angularity. Many people had a hand in this long process, and it is surely natural to assume that they would have included both men and women.

Because it was used primarily by women, the new script was called *onna-de* "women's hand" as opposed to Chinese characters, which were *otoko-de* "men's hand." It played an active role as the medium for Heian women's literature, which was to enter its full glory with *Genji monogatari*. Thus, the development of *hiragana* ushered in the golden age of women's literature mentioned earlier in our brief review of literary history.

In this golden age, Sei Shōnagon produced her collection of occasional writings with its flashes of wit and mordant insights. Murasaki Shikibu wrote her great romance, and although it is the world's oldest, the psychology of its characters, their conflicts and passions, are still fresh today. Women of the court also recorded deep reflections and frank confessions in many famous diaries, such as the *Kagerō nikki* (ca. 982; tr. The Gossamer Years), *Izumi Shikibu nikki* (1007; The Izumi Shikibu Diary), and *Sarashina nikki* (ca 1060; tr. As I Crossed a Bridge of Dreams).

During this time men were writing works in Chinese, as represented by the poetry anthologies *Kaifūsō* (751), *Ryōunshō* (814), and Sugawara no Michizane's poetry collection *Kankebunsō* (900). Since the writers were expressing themselves in what was, after all, a foreign language, it was difficult for them to produce works of intrinsic worth. This is clearly reflected by the paucity of works by male authors of the 11th century in the literary chronology cited earlier.

Men were later to join women in writing literary prose in *kana*, influenced by their continual output of works of the highest quality. Official documents were still written in *kanbun*, however, and until the late Edo period, that is, the mid-19th century, there would continue to be two parallel tracks: Chinese characters and *kanbun* for the public, mainstream, and male-dominated spheres, and Japanese prose and *hiragana* for the private, secondary, and female-oriented spheres.

Today, the standard Japanese orthography, whether for public or private texts, poetry or prose, is *kanji-kana-majiribun*, a mixture of *kanji* and *kana* in which nouns and the roots of verbs and adjectives are written in Chinese characters, while the syntactic framework of particles and inflectional endings is written in *hiragana*. Thus, the script that was steadily used and refined by women has come to form the backbone of written expression in Japanese.

ATTITUDES TO WOMEN'S SPEECH IN THE HEIAN PERIOD

How was women's use of the spoken language perceived in Heian society? Here, too, *Genji monogatari* and *Makura no sōshi* will serve as our main sources of information.

In the passage quoted earlier from "The Broom Tree" in *Genji monogatari*, the explanation given by the woman who was too fond of using Chinese words is said to have "poured forth at great length, all of it very well reasoned" (Seidensticker, p. 36). Both her rapid speech and her logical presentation are ridiculed here, which suggests that neither was favored in a woman.

In volume 26, "Wild Carnations," a woman character named the Lady of Ōmi appears. To the discomfiture of Tō no Chūjō and his family, she announces herself as his daughter, born to a woman of undistinguished lineage. Murasaki describes her as having grown up among country people and not knowing the proper way to speak. Her speech is described as being much too fast, her voice as shrill, and her diction as overemphatic, accented, and very inelegant. In contrast, Murasaki describes the following ideal: "Pure, precise speech can give a certain distinction to rather ordinary remarks. An impromptu poem, for instance, if it is spoken musically, with an air at the beginning and end as of something unsaid, can seem to convey worlds of meaning, even if upon mature reflection it does not seem to have said much of anything at all" (Seidensticker, p. 451; Arthur Waley gives "a quiet, colourless voice" for "[p]ure precise speech" [1957–58, 521]). In volume 29, "The Royal Outing," Tō no Chūjō makes fun of the Ōmi lady's oddly emphatic way of speaking, and the women attendants behind the curtains have difficulty restraining their laughter at her most unladylike exuberance.

Murasaki Shikibu—or, rather, the society in which she lived—apparently considered it appropriate for a woman's speech to be calm and quiet, and the beginning and end of her utterances not too well-defined. On the other hand, speaking quickly, emphatically, or logically was considered unbecoming.

In section 182 [177] of *Makura no sōshi*, Sei Shōnagon describes

19

Korechika, the Major Counselor, and the ladies-in-waiting joking together. The women, she says, "replied without the slightest embarrassment, freely arguing with him and contradicting his remarks when they disagreed. I was absolutely dazzled by it all and found myself blushing without any particular reason" (Morris 1967, 180). In section 210 [206], she lists "Things That Should Be Short":

> A piece of thread when one wants to sew something in a hurry.
> A lamp stand.
> The hair of a woman of the lower classes should be neat and short.
> The speech of a young girl. (Morris 1967, 195)

In other words, Sei Shōnagon found it quite shameful for a woman to argue with a man, and preferred an unmarried woman's speech to be short.

Thus, although no gender differences were seen in the areas of vocabulary and grammar, the works of Murasaki Shikibu and Sei Shōnagon do contain evidence of various social constraints on women's use of language and manner of speech.

WOMEN'S SOCIAL STATUS

The emergence of many such constraints on women's speech, unknown in the Nara period, was a reflection of the changing social status of Heian women. At this point I would like to briefly trace the status of women from ancient times to the Heian period.

Ancient Japanese society was matrilineal,[8] and the mother was central to family organization. The highest deity in Japanese mythology was a goddess, Amaterasu-ōmikami. Archaeological findings have established the existence of women rulers in the Kofun period (ca. 300–710) in various parts of Japan, and in the fudoki, the collections of reports on regional geography, products, and oral traditions, which were compiled around 715, the volume for Harima, now part of Hyōgo prefecture, records that there were two female chieftains known as Harimatome and Tambatome.

The most powerful of the many local clans founded the Yamato Court, the precursor of the imperial dynastic line, in what is now Nara prefecture and this line included female rulers. Where the earliest emperors are concerned, the boundary between myth and historical fact is unclear, and their reigns cannot be dated by the Western calendar. Historical dates can, however, be assigned to twenty-four imperial reigns from that of Emperor Keitai (507–31) to the end of the Nara period (794), and of these twenty-four, eight were the reigns of empresses who ruled for a total of ninety years. (There were actually six empresses, two of them having acceded twice to the throne.) There were no empresses during the Heian period, and no woman was to occupy the throne for another 800 years, until the two figurehead empresses of the Edo period, who, as puppets of the Tokugawa shogunate, held no real power.

The *Man'yōshū* is believed to have been compiled at the behest of the Empresses Jitō, Genmei, and Genshō, three of the six Nara-period empresses, who were rulers in fact as well as in name. From the end of the Nara period onward, women's role in the court was diminished, and they came to be excluded from the center of politics. This was a result of the gradual permeation of Japanese society by the Chinese Confucian thought and its concepts of male dominance, which lay behind the Taihō Code (promulgated in 701). Coupled with these changing attitudes was the spread of the concept of female impurity, in which menstruation and childbirth were regarded as unclean. The gods of the *Kojiki* did not view menstruation as unclean, but by the beginning of the Heian period, there were records of the imperial princesses who served at Ise Shrine undergoing ritual purification in a river. There is also a record of the imperial princesses who served at the Kamo Shrines being removed from the performance of religious rites during their menstrual periods.

It was these views of women as inferior and unclean that combined to gradually exclude women from the political arena. Even the *naishi no kami*, the chief ladies-in-waiting, who in the Nara period had served the emperors in an important advisory role, were gradually reduced to serving them in private life only.

Meanwhile, an intense power struggle was developing among the nobility, centered on the imperial succession. One way for an aristocrat to gain a hold on political power was to have his daughter become a consort to the emperor and bear him a son. Rivalry among the consorts was intense, for in order to attract the emperor's eye and become the mother of the crown prince, a woman needed more than good looks. She also needed to be accomplished in poetry, music, and calligraphy.

Women like Sei Shōnagon and Murasaki Shikibu, who could serve as tutors to these daughters of the nobility were in great demand. Thus the early 11th century, when the struggle for political power was at its height, also witnessed the first great flowering of literature created by women.

With the decline of the court aristocracy and the rise of the warrior class, Japan became a masculine society, and women's works would not make another appearance in the chronology of literary history until the late 19th century.

NOTES

1. Saeki reports that the gender difference disappeared during the Heian period as male use of *kimi* increased. This form of address is still in general use today, but in modern usage it is a masculine term. From the Meiji period (1868–1912) until the beginning of the Shōwa period (1926–89), it was regarded as inappropriate for women's speech.

2. Unless otherwise indicated, all quotations from classical Japanese texts are from the *Nihon no koten* (Japanese Classics) series published by Shōgakkan; herein referred to as "the Shōgakkan text."

3. Except where otherwise noted, all quoted passages from *Genji monogatari* are from the translation by Edward Seidensticker (Knopf, 1976). The names of characters in English are also taken from Seidensticker's translation.

4. For a closer look at the state of women's writing in the 20th century, Table 2 shows the gender of recipients of the Akutagawa Prize. Established in 1935 and presented twice yearly to relatively unknown writers of prose fiction, this award is regarded as the gateway to success in Japan's literary world. Over its 60-year history, it has been awarded in a ratio of women to men averaging 23:100. Recently however, this has been increasing; the average since 1975 (International Women's Year) is 37.5:100.

Table 2. Comparison of winners of Akutagawa Prize by gender

	Male	Female
Total: 1935-1993	110	25
1935-1944	19	2
1945-1974 (postwar years)	51	8
1975-1993 (post-IWY)	40	15

5. Princess Uchiko, daughter of Emperor Saga (who reigned 809–23).

6. The collected works of the Tang-dynasty poet Bo Juyi (Po Chū-i, 772–846), and the anthology *Wen xuan*, a collection of poetry and prose from the Chou to the Liang dynasty, compiled by Prince Shōmei (501–31 A.D.).

7. In a note to this passage, Ivan Morris explains: "Although Shōnagon knows the following line ... perfectly well, she prefers to avoid Chinese characters, the so-called 'men's writing' (*otoko-moji*). Instead she uses the *kana* script to write the last two lines (7-7 syllables) of a Japanese poem on the same theme ... To understand why Shōnagon's reply ... was so successful we must remember that Chinese literature, even the poetry of such a popular writer as Po Chū-I, was supposed to be beyond women's ken. To send a Chinese poem to a woman was most unconventional; that is why Shōnagon was at a complete loss" (vol. 2, pp. 66–67, n. 337).

8. The recent consensus among historians appears to be that "at the present stage no conclusion can be reached as to whether the society was matrilineal, colineal, or patrilineal" (Wakita Haruko et al., *Nihon joseishi* [Yoshikawa kōbunkan, 1992], p. 13).

CHAPTER 2
WOMEN'S LANGUAGE IN THE KAMAKURA AND MUROMACHI PERIODS: ACTUALIZATION OF GENDERED LANGUAGE DIFFERENCES

In this chapter, I will discuss women and language from the twelfth to the early 17th century, that is, the medieval period, which was dominated by samurai and a male-oriented culture. During this time, women lost much of their earlier status in society, and their linguistic patterns changed. This discussion will draw on examples from *Heike monogatari* (The Tale of the Heike) and *kyōgen* (comic one-act plays) and will look as well at attitudes towards women's language contained in essays from the period. The central focus of the discussion will be *nyōbō-kotoba*, the language of the court ladies, which came into existence during that time.

THE LIVES OF WOMEN IN THE MEDIEVAL PERIOD

Japanese women's history has attracted an increasing amount of scholarly attention in recent years, and some scholars are beginning to disagree with the common view that medieval women were oppressed under the feudal system. Tabata Yasuko (1996) maintains that the political power of medieval women such as Hōjō Masako and Hino Tomiko was equal to that of their husbands, Minamoto Yoritomo and Ashikaga Yoshimasa. As typical women of the samurai class, they did more than merely obey their husbands (Tabata 1996, 22).

However, even if this was the case for prominent women and women from the upper samurai classes, most women of the period suffered numerous restraints and severe oppression, due to the influence of the type of Buddhist teachings that prevailed in the Kamakura and Muromachi periods.

In medieval Buddhism, women were considered sinful beings that impeded men's efforts to follow the Buddhist path. Buddhism did not, however, disparage women when it was first transmitted to Japan at the beginning of the 6th century because shamanism was deeply entrenched in the indigenous culture. In the 7th and 8th centuries, many women renounced the world to become nuns. These women were highly regarded, so much so that Buddhist nunneries were built along side Buddhist monasteries.

In the Kamakura period (1192–1333) highly influential monks such as Shinran (1173–1262) and Nichiren (1222–82) popularized Buddhism among the common people. As Buddhist scriptures became well known and Buddhist teachings spread, their intrinsic contempt for women gained currency in Japanese society, leading to discrimination against women.

Tsuma kagami (1300; The Mirror for Wives), a collection of works by Mujū (1226–1312), a monk of the Rinzai sect, contains the following account:

> Human beings are foolish. It is written throughout the scriptures that women in particular are very sinful. *Nanzan no Senritsushi* states that women are guilty of seven sins. The first is causing men to feel sexual desire; the second is being prone to jealousy; the third is lying, so that what they say with their mouths differs from what they think in their hearts; the fourth is being vain and greedy; the fifth is telling many lies and not much truth; the sixth is burning with desire and knowing no shame; the seventh is having impure bodies and passing blood often. . . . (*NKBT* 83, 121)

Mujū goes on to explain that for these reasons women must devote themselves to Buddhist teachings: "If women are aware of the gravity of their sins, they should repent and give up the riches and honor of this life of illusion and devote themselves to a life of Buddhist asceticism that would save their souls for all eternity." Views such as his took root in medieval society.

Abutsuni (died 1283) was one of the few female writers of the Kamakura period. Her well-known work, *Izayoi nikki* (1279) is a travel diary based on the trial for rights to her deceased husband's estate, in which she fought the heir to the estate on behalf of her own daughter. Abutsuni also wrote *Niwa no oshie* (The Teachings of the Garden), otherwise known as *Menoto no fumi* (The Nursemaid Letters, 1283), for her daughter, explaining the way in which a woman should live. The work contains the following passages:

> Even if something happily meets your expectations, you should not say, "How delightful!" or "How fortunate!" You should be vague and noncommittal in regard to both oneself and others. Do not show your emotions. You should not speak rashly, whatever the circumstances. . . . The verses women compose should not be grandiloquent, but charming and gentle. . . . Practice your characters over and over again, and write them beautifully. . . . Even a few characters can reveal one's nature and what is in one's heart, too. (*NKBJH* 1910, 11)

On the other hand, in *Chikubashō* (1383), one of a number of instruction texts written for samurai warriors of the medieval period, the author Shiba Yoshimasa (1350–1410) writes that "(n)ot becoming angry at things that should anger one, not saying what one finds reproachful and grievous, not giving rein to one's feelings of vengeance and then being thought of as compliant by others—these are all things that will bring one's downfall" (Saeki 1942, 242). Shiba's teachings are exactly opposite from those that Abutsuni advocates. While Abutsuni advises self-restraint, Shiba Yoshimasa advises self-assertion. Abutsuni's advice to women to shun grandiloquence and practice charm, even when composing *waka*, illustrates that society prefers women who are unassertive and charming.

Menoto no sōshi (The Nursemaid Book, early 14th century), a book of instruction for women serving at court, gives the following advice regarding the speech and manners of young girls:

> When a girl becomes ten years of age, take her deep into the chambers and ensure that she is not seen by others. Keep her in a calm frame of mind, and raise her to speak in a soft, low voice. Do not allow her to play as she pleases, to speak roughly, or to sprawl about near the veranda. (*NKBJH* 1910, 35)

In the ninth passage of the *Tsurezuregusa* (Essays in Idleness), the most famous anthology of essays from the medieval period, the author Yoshida Kenkō (1283–1352) writes, "Women lead others astray with their mere presence. No matter who the woman is, one is not able to relax and sleep deeply. It is only out of lust that they endure things they should not withstand, showing no regard for themselves" (*NKBT* 1957, 96). Yoshida continues, in passage 107, saying that women are shallow and stupid.

> In fact, women are all perverse by nature. They are deeply self-centered, grasping in the extreme, devoid of all susceptibility to reason, quick to indulge in superstitious practice. They are clever talkers, but may refuse to utter a word when asked even some perfectly unobjectionable question. One might suppose this meant they were cautious, but they are equally apt to discuss, quite unsolicited, matters being passed over in silence. Their ingenuity in embroidering their stories is too much for the wisdom of any man, but when, presently, their fictions are exposed, they never perceive it. Women are devious but stupid. (Keene 1967, 90)

The author of *Mi no katami*, believed to be Ichijō Kanera (1402–81), a politician and scholar of the Muromachi period, suggests that women are devilish: "Women are the kin of Dairokuten no maō, the Sixth King of the Demons, and they became women to prevent men from following Buddhism. For it is written in the sutras 'even if one might look upon a serpent monster, one must not look upon a woman'" (*NKBJH* 1910, 62).

Women's very existence is contemptuously regarded as sinful. Men, on the other hand, are superior because of their manhood and must be revered. The text continues: "Man is the incarnation of many Buddhas past, present, and future. A man may appear more vulgar than oneself, yet do not think poorly of him. He is correct in judgment of right and wrong, and full of mercy. One must never treat a man without respect."

Women, as those who must serve men—men being the reincarnations of deities—must be modest in their daily actions and take particular care in how they speak. Women are given the following warnings: "Young women should not laugh in loud voices when at the bathhouse or elsewhere. They especially should exercise care not to tell jokes."

As instructed by Buddhist teachings, these poets, monks, and scholars believed women to be intrinsically sinful and of less worth than men. They therefore instruct women to pay men due respect and be careful in their speech and actions.

MEDIEVAL WOMEN'S LANGUAGE

It is difficult to ascertain exactly how women in the medieval period spoke. In chapter 1 we used the dialogues from *Genji monogatari*, and in the present chapter we have no recourse other than to employ existing historical literary texts—written versions of spoken language. These texts may differ greatly from the actual spoken language of the time, but they indicate the way in which people of the time altered their language use according to their addressee, and therefore, they allow us to consider elements common to all speakers.

Let us first look at the conversations contained in *Konjaku monogatari shū* (Tales of Times Now Past), a collection of stories compiled around the middle of the 12th century. In the collection, the twenty-sixth story is about the formation of islands in Tosa, present-day Kōchi prefecture [10] (*NKBT* 1962, 444). A man of humble rank tends to a rice paddy at a bay a small distance from his beachside home. One day, he travels to the paddy in his boat, and just as he beaches the vessel and begins to prepare to plant rice, the boat is washed out to sea with his fourteen-year-old son and twelve-year-old daughter still aboard. The boat is blown across to a faraway island. With no way to get home, the children burst into tears, but the girl says, "There is nothing we can do. But still, we shouldn't throw our lives away. As long as we have food, we can eat it bit by bit and keep ourselves alive. Yet, once this has gone, how will we survive? I know, let's plant this seedling before it dries up." The boy replies, "Undoubtedly, you are right, let's do as you say.

Without doubt." And they begin making a rice paddy.

Both the boy and the girl speak with equal cordiality, perhaps because this is a conversation between children. Note that it is the younger sister who is levelheaded and leads her older brother.

Passage 31 [10] of *Konjaku monogatari shū* (*NKBT* 1963, 265) contains an argument between a husband who frequently visits his lover, and his wife who correctly guesses what is happening. The wife says, "What a shameless man you are. The smug look on your face after going to that woman's house and sleeping with her." To which the husband says, "Who said such a thing?" And the wife replies, "How detestable, I saw it clearly in my dream." Both husband and wife speak without honorifics and use the same level of language, most likely because they are engaged in an argument.

Passage 30 [9] (*NKBT* 1963, 236) is famous for the *ubasute* legend, which tells of abandoning old people to die. A wife, who considers her husband's elderly aunt to be a burden, says to her husband, "Your aunt's disposition is detestable. Take her deep into the mountains and get rid of her." At first, the husband ignores her, but after being reproached again and again by his wife, he decides to abandon his aunt. He says to his aunt, "Let us depart, dear Aunt. I wish to show you an edifying service to take place at the temple." The wife does not use honorifics when speaking to her husband, but the husband uses a high level of honorifics when speaking to his aunt. In these dialogues, we witness not a gender difference of women addressing men politely, but an age difference, in which younger people address older family members with respect.

Needless to say, there are many examples where women use honorifics in addressing men, but men do not use honorifics at all. Let us look at the "Giō" (*NKBT* 1959, 96) chapter from *Heike monogatari*, in which the dancer Hotoke Gozen has gained a reputation in the capital but despite her fame has not been summoned by the leader of the Taira, Chancellor-Novice Kiyomori. She arrives unannounced at his quarters and directly asks for an audience with him. Upon being told of her arrival by his servants, Kiyomori is angered. "What is this? Entertainers like her are not supposed to present themselves without being summoned. What makes her think she can simply show up like this? She is not god or Buddha[1] and thus has no business coming to a place where Giō is staying. Throw her out at once" (McCullough 1988, 31).

Upon hearing this, Giō tries desperately to intervene. "It is quite the usual thing for an entertainer to present herself without an invitation. Then, too, they say Hotoke is still very young. It would be cruel to send her home with that harsh dismissal, now that she has ventured to come here. As a dancer myself, I cannot help feeling involved: I would be uncomfortable

27

and sad, too. You would be doing her a great kindness by at least receiving her before sending her away, even if you don't watch her dance or listen to her sing. Won't you please be a little lenient and call her back to be received?" (McCullough 1988, 31). Giō pleads, and Kiyomori replies, "Well, my dear, since you make a point of it, I'll see her before she goes."

The language Kiyomori uses to Hotoke and Giō is completely lacking in honorifics and represents that of the most powerful men. On the other hand, Giō, who is now in the service of the most powerful man in the capital, speaks as a woman in a humble position, being a former courtesan like Hotoke. Her language features an abundance of the most polite honorific forms. This example illustrates how social power is reflected in language use.

In the section of *Heike monogatari* called "Shigehira no Kirare" (*NKBT* 1960, 374) ("The Execution of Shigehira") [11], there is a scene where the captured Shigehira catches a glimpse of his wife in Hino as he is being transported to Nara. The following is the exchange between Shigehira and his wife.

"Your clothes look so shabby," the lady[2] said. "Please change into something else." She produced a wadded, short-sleeved robe and a white hunting robe, and Shigehira put them on. He left his old robes with her. "Look on them as a keepsake." . . . . Shigehira moved to leave. "Those who exchange vows are certain of meeting in the life to come. Pray that we may be reborn on the same lotus blossom. The sun is low and the way to Nara is long; I do not want to keep the warriors waiting" (McCullough 1988, 398–99). In this exchange, this noble samurai-class husband and wife both use a high level of honorifics when conversing with each other.

Hosshin shū (*SNK* 1976, 183) (Collection of tales of religious awakening), a text from the early 13th century, is a collection of Buddhist anecdotes about how commoners, nobility, and samurai gained their faith. The use of honorifics in these tales depends on differences in social class, rather than on gender. In the story "A Court Lady, Seeing Demons on her Death Bed," Hijiri visits the death bed of a court lady and attempts to soothe her distress. Hijiri asks, "What do you see?" To which the lady replies, "Many fearful creatures are approaching with fire." Hijiri admonishes her saying, "Firmly believe that Amida Buddha will save you, and steadfastly recite '*Namu Amida Butsu*' (Hail Amida Buddha)." After a short while the lady speaks, "The fire is out. A carriage decorated with jewels carrying many celestial nymphs playing instruments has come for me."

In this section, Hijiri uses the honorific verb *tamau*, "deign to," and expresses respect, yet the lady does not use any form of honorific. Hijiri is in a high social position, but since the lady is a member of the imperial court, a daughter of the Emperor, her social standing is relatively higher.

The examples above show that speech from this period expresses differences in social class in the same way that Heian speech does, but that there are no unambiguous examples of gendered speech. Among the nobility and samurai in the capital, differences in social position are expressed by the absence or presence of honorific language. We may assume that commoners, both men and women, spoke identically to each other.

WOMEN AS DEPICTED IN *KYŌGEN*

Kyōgen[3] were a popular form of entertainment in the medieval period, and works from this genre provide glimpses of society's attitudes towards women in the 16th and 17th centuries. In a play called *Okosako*, a wife reproaches her husband at the end of an argument saying, "You beast of a man, you beast of a man!" Her husband angrily replies, "You can put a pair of eyes and a nose on a chopstick, but a man is still a man! How is it you come to call your husband a beast!" Similarly in *Oka-dayū*, a wife knowledgeable about Chinese poetry makes allusions to it when explaining it, but the explanations go over her husband's head. She becomes angry at her husband's ignorance and contemptuously says to him, "Did you swill the wine?" using the slightly vulgar expression *kurau*, "devour." In response, her husband beats her saying, "Even if he is made of straw, a man still is a man. So how do you come to ask me if I devoured my food or not?"[4] The common essence of these two *kyōgen* lines is that a man is always important, simply because he is a man. That is to say, "a man is still a man," and, therefore, a woman has no right to disparage him, no matter how much of a good-for-nothing he is, and no matter how superior she is.

In another *kyōgen* play, *Hikkukuri*, a husband fed up with his wife seizes the opportunity of his wife's visit to her parents to send a servant with a letter of divorce. In a similar scene in *Inabadō*, a husband says, "My wife was drinking a lot, being unreasonable with me, and not doing any housework. It was extremely annoying, so I sent her a letter of divorce when she happened to be at her parents' home."

These two examples give us a picture of a society that allowed husbands to divorce their wives unilaterally. Most divorces occurred because men felt that their wives despised them and were not docilely obedient. Although we can imagine women as spirited survivors, this was a very male-dominated world overall. Unlike the examples from *Konjaku monogatari shū* above, where neither wife nor husband uses honorifics, conversations found in *kyōgen* clearly show women addressing their husbands with honorific language.

For example, in *Kagami otoko*, the husband says, *"Ika ni mo midomo mo zuibun sokusai de modotta ga, sonata mo kawaru koto mo noute medetō oryaru"*

(I, myself, have returned without incident, and it is good to find you also unchanged). The wife then replies, *"Nani ga sate, warawa mo kawaru koto mo gozaranu. Sate konata no gososhō no koto wa nan to nari*mashite gozaruzo" (In any event, I never change. Incidentally, how did the matter of your appeal fare?) (author's emphasis). In this dialogue, the husband uses honorific language only once in describing his wife's state of being, *oryaru*. In contrast, the wife uses the honorific prefix *go* to refer to her husband's appeal and also uses the polite language forms *narimashite* (becoming), *gozaranu* (negative form of copula), and *gozaru zo* (interrogative form of copula).

Gender differentiation in the spoken language became distinct in the medieval period. *Kokonchomonjū* (1254), a collection of stories from the Kamakura period, contains the following comment: "In making replies, men say *'yo'* and women say *'wo'"* (*SNK* 1983, 404). In other words, this states that people of the same high status reply differently depending on whether they are male or female.

Menoto no sōshi, quoted from earlier, also touches upon how replies should be made, but here we find a more elaborate formulation concerning the nature of appropriate replies: "There are three ways for a woman to reply. To her parents, she says *wo*. When she meets an equal, she answers with *ya*. To an inferior, she answers *ei*." This indicates that language differentiation according to both social status and gender had been established, and that women were supposed to address their parents in the same way that they addressed superiors. Furthermore, a female speaker could be addressed using a variety of language styles depending on the status of the addresser. Gender differentiation is notable in the use of first person pronouns. *Soregashi, warera, ware,* and *mi* were in the main part of men's speech, and *wagami mizukara* and *warawa* were part of women's speech.

As for why this gender differentiation occurred, Hasegawa Nyoze-kan explains that "entering the age of the samurai, the Japanese language began to take on the masculine pitch of the Kanto dialect and in connection with this shift, the use of words of Chinese origin, which were also perceived as masculine language, became more common" (Hasegawa 1943, 119). We can say with certainty that gender differentiation in language is closely related to the maintenance of political power by the samurai and the establishment of male dominance.

THE FORMATION OF *NYŌBŌ-KOTOBA* — THE LANGUAGE OF WOMEN AT COURT

In the society of medieval Japan, the shogunate and the samurai class as a whole held the real power, while the emperor had only limited powers. The imperial court, consisting of the emperor, retired emperors, ministers, vice ministers and so on supplemented the power of the shogunate and was responsible for law administration and protocol. The imperial system also put great effort into preservation and transmission of traditional culture. Women who worked within this system, particularly those who attended the imperial family and high ministers in their daily affairs, were known as *nyōbō*. In general, they were daughters of the nobility and high-class intellectuals.

The *nyōbō* gave new names to everyday items and behaviors and used those new terms as references when speaking within the group. The majority of names were allotted to food and drinks; for example, steamed rice was called *kugo* instead of *gohan*, water was called *ohiya* instead of *mizu*, sushi was called *sumoji*, and tofu was referred to as *kabe*. New names were also given to personal belongings. The *nyōbō* also used a unique set of adjectives, such as *hamoji* instead of *hazukashii* for "shameful," and verbs, such as *hirou* instead of *aruku* for "walk." According to Mashimo (1948) 17 such words are recorded in the Muromachi period text *Amanomokuzu* (Collection of Customs, 1420), and 129 in *Ōjorō onnanokoto* (Matters of the Court Women), a total of 146 such expressions. If we add in the words found in *Oyudononoue no nikki* (The Diaries of Oyudononoue) (1477–1826), the diary kept by the *nyōbō* at court for over 200 years, the total is approximately 300 terms. These terms are collectively referred to as *nyōbō-kotoba* in *Oyudono-noue no nikki*, and I shall refer to them as such from this point onward.

The question that begs to be asked is why the *nyōbō* created an argot composed of new names for common items? As we will discuss in chapter 6, it is common for members of a group to use language that outsiders cannot understand. Students enjoy making up and using expressions that are understood only on campus. People in the same profession or workplace use in-group jargon. Department store clerks use expressions not easily understood by customers to tell each other that they are going to the toilet. The military, too, has its own unique words and expressions.

The examples mentioned above are all kinds of argots: language used exclusively among members of a specific group to foster closer relationships and unity within the group while at the same time weakening relationships with those on the outside. Like students who jokingly create new expressions, the *nyōbō* most likely started using expressions that others would not understand simply for amusement. Yet, why was a secret language necessary?

Let us summarize the views of Sugimoto Tsutomu, Horii Reiichi, Morino Muneaki, and Hattori Yoshika, all specialists in the language of the *nyōbō*.

31

Unlike dealings with commoners, dealings with nobles required courtiers to act with composure and elegance. Straightforward language use was not permitted, and etiquette demanded that women, in particular, use elegant, refined, and indirect language (Hattori 1954, 110). Beginning in the Nanbokuchō period (14th century), contact between courtiers and the masses increased, and as a result, food and drink consumed by commoners found its way onto the tables of the nobility, who considered it vulgar to call food by the same names that commoners used (Horii 1990, 34). Essentially, speaking of food openly was considered undignified, and something to be avoided, particularly in front of those to whom one owed deference (Hattori 1954, 110). The creation, refinement, and command of *nyōbō kotoba* was an ostentatious way to display the group's culture and learning and was a sign of their privileged position. In other words, the *nyōbō* showed their superiority through language use, affirming themselves and protecting their sense of identity (Morino 1991, 234).

Another view holds that *nyōbō kotoba* was an artificial language born of the need for communication among social classes. Sugimoto states that "it is to be expected that women of the lower classes and working women who went in and out of the imperial palace would end up sharing a common language at their work places when working together. It can be thought of as a type of linguistic innovation, whereby accents and so forth are subsumed into a common code" (Sugimoto 1967, 744).

With the understanding that the language of the *nyōbō* arose for some of the reasons cited above, let us now look in depth at the language itself. The methods of word formation that obtained in *nyōbō kotoba* can be categorized in the following patterns:

> (1) Addition of the honorific prefix *o* to existing words. Omission of the end of a word is sometimes encountered, and the addition of *mi* is also seen. Some of these words are still in use today and are marked by an asterisk.
>
> > *imo* "potato" -> *o-imo**
> > *yu* "hot water" -> *o-yu**
> > *sakana* "side dishes" -> *o-sakana**
> > *dengaku* "bean curd grilled and coated with miso" ->
> > > *o-den**
> > *manjū* "cake" -> *o-man*
> > *miyage* "souvenir" -> *o-miya*
> > *ashi* "leg, foot" -> *o-mi-ashi**
> > *obi* "sash" -> *o-mi-obi*
>
> (2) Abbreviation of existing words:
> > takenoko "bamboo shoot" -> *take*
> > matsutake "pine mushroom" -> *matsu*

      <u>manj</u>ū "cake" -> *man*
      <u>konnyaku</u> "devil's root paste" -> *nyaku*
      chi<u>maki</u> "rice dumpling wrapped in bamboo leaves" ->
           maki
      <u>gob</u>ō "burdock root" -> *gon*

(3) Addition of *moji* to abbreviations of existing words:
      <u>ka</u>mi "hair" -> *ka-moji**
      <u>shin</u>pai "worry" -> *shin-moji*
      <u>su</u>shi "vinegared rice" -> *su-moji*
      <u>so</u>nata "you" -> *so-moji*
      <u>ta</u>ko "octopus" -> *ta-moji*
      <u>mu</u>gi "wheat" -> *mu-moji*
      <u>ome</u> ni kakaru "to meet" -> *ome-moji**

(4) Addition of *mono* to words related in concept to existing words:
      na "greens" -> *ao-mono** "green things, greens"
      udon "thick white noodles" -> *o-naga-mono* "long things"
      gekkei "menstruation, period" -> *tsuki no mono** "thing of
           the month, monthly thing"
      shio "salt" -> *shiro-mono* "white thing"
      nabe "pot" -> *kuro-mono* "black thing"

(5) Creation of words conceptually related to the characteristic color, shape, and/or nature of the original words:
      iwashi "sardine" -> *murasaki* (purple)
      azuki "adzuki beans, red beans" -> *aka* "red," *oaka*
           "honorable red"
      tōfu "bean curd" -> *kabe* "wall," *o-kabe* "honorable wall"
      sōmen "thin noodles" -> *hoso-mono* "thin things," *shiraito*
           "white threads"
      konuka "rice bran" -> *machikane* "waiting impatiently"
      mizu "cold water" -> *o-hiya** "honorable cold"
      ohiyashi "honorable cooled thing"
      yamadori "copper pheasant" -> *ashibiki* (a word used as a
           poetic epithet for *yamadori* in poetry.)

(6) Addition of words or syllables to parts of existing words or conceptually related words:
      azuki "adzuki beans, red beans" -> *aka-aka* "red-red"
      irimame "toasted beans" -> *iri-iri* (repetition of beginning
           of word)
      kazunoko "herring roe" -> *kazu-kazu* (repetition of
           beginning of word)
      dango "dumpling" -> *ishi-ishi* "yummy-yummy"
      nigiyaka "lively" -> *nigi-nigi* (repetition of beginning of
           word)

(7) Avoidance of the Chinese pronunciation of words of Chinese origin:

> *kaji* "fire" -> *akagoto* "red thing"
> *kinsu* "gold currency" -> *kogane* "gold metal"
> *ginsu* "silver currency" -> *kurogane* "black money"
> *sekihan* "rice cooked with red beans" -> *akakowaii* "red firm steamed rice"
> *tenkyo* "moving house" -> *watamashi* "going over"
> *henji* "answer" -> *irae* (indigenous Japanese word for "answer")

The use of the honorific *o* in group one adds elegance, indirectness, and politeness. The prefix *o* can also be added to words formed using methods from pattern two onwards. The other patterns involve the addition of extra syllables or lexical substitution, which makes the language difficult for outsiders to understand. In patterns three and four, the addition of *mono* or *moji* to existing words effectively softens them, and the general affix *mono* "thing" in particular results in a more ambiguous expression. This is a euphemistic manner of speech that does not express things frankly or directly.

An element of playfulness can be seen in the expressions of group five, which are formed from conceptually related words and give us an idea of the *nyōbō* sense of humor. Calling *iwashi* "sardines," *murasaki* "purple," reflects the sentiment that sardines taste better than *ayu* "sweetfish," and the word play hinges on the pronunciation of *ayu* as *ai*, which also means "indigo." The supposed superiority of the color purple over indigo was considered similar to the superiority of sardines over sweetfish. Similarly, the expression *machikane* for *konuka*, "rice bran" is said to have come about because *mada konuka* "hasn't it come yet?" is conceptually related to *machikaneru* "to wait impatiently."

The abbreviations seen in group two are similar to abbreviations used in baby talk, and they are not polite expressions, because shortening existing words to spare oneself the trouble of pronouncing them does not elevate the person addressed. Using only the end of the word as an abbreviation, as in the cases of *nyaku* for *konnyaku*, "devil's root paste," and *maki* for *chimaki*, "rice dumplings wrapped in bamboo leaves," is a method common in the speech of young people today, who abbreviate the place names Ikebukuro and Shinjuku as *Bukuro* and *Juku*. However, these modern abbreviated forms are considered not elegant but corrupt. Furthermore, it should be noted that the addition of the phoneme "*n*" to "*go*" of *gobō*, "burdock root," to form *gon* produces a heavy, strong-sounding term. Although easy to pronounce, it cannot be considered aesthetically pleasing.

Expressions listed in category six above also share similarities with baby talk, which relies heavily on repetition. It is thought the *nyōbō*, adults themselves, created many of these expressions because they had frequent contact with the children of the court. Moreover, it is possible that the social standards of the day considered childish-sounding language used by women to be attractive or charming.

Expressions listed in category seven reflect the tradition carried on from the Heian period that discouraged women from using all but a few Chinese characters and words of Chinese origin. Words of Chinese origin contain many voiced consonants and palatalized and labio-velar elements, which were not considered suitable for women, whose speech was required to be quiet and soft-spoken.

We have seen that frequent use of the honorific prefix *o* in polite expressions, and the employment of vague and indirect euphemisms are characteristic qualities of *nyōbō-kotoba*. From this we can conclude *nyōbō-kotoba* is, on the one hand, refined and elegant, but on the other, awkward, naïve, and childish. In the past, the beauty and elegance of the language of female court attendants was not questioned, and the style was considered to represent refined speech. Sugimoto writes, "The women's language that flowered during the turmoil of the wars is a collection of masterpieces that merit more than a thousand words of praise each" (1985b, 157). Kikuzawa comments, "They tried to show the female characteristic of refinement in many ways, through politeness, beauty, and elegance, and through the use of euphemisms and avoidance of foreign loan words" (1940, 272). Furthermore, Yoshida Sumio maintains that "women's language gives the impression of elegance and refinement" (1952a, 33), and that the most representative of this style is the language of the *nyōbō*.

However, as we have seen earlier, *nyōbō* language was not always considered elegant and refined. In the Edo period, in fact, some went so far as to deplore it. One scholar even condemned it as "disgraceful." Scholar and *tanka* poet Tayasu Munetake (1715–71) lamented in *Kusamusubi* (Concluding Notes), "It is the way of the world that people's language should change, but nothing is more appalling than the speech of women. They rephrase fine old expressions in dreadful new terms and convert beautiful old phrases into ones of Chinese origin. Such language use can be forgiven if the new word replaces a coarse term, but it is extremely disturbing that these new words are worse than those previously used" (Kunida 1964, 693).

Tayasu gives the use of *aka* "red" for *azuki* as an actual example, commenting that "Because adzuki beans are red, small children who are not yet able to remember many words are taught to call them *aka*, but I do not understand why one should keep on using this expression once one has become an adult." As for calling *miso* "bean paste" *mushi* "steamed," he says,

"Commoners believe that *miso* is probably called *mushi* because they steam it when making it." Moreover, in regard to the use of *gon* for *gobō*, "burdock root," he says, "Women based this expression on the word *gonbō*, the word used for *gobō* by men of low birth with rough accents." Clearly, therefore, Tayasu regards *nyōbō-kotoba* as vulgar.

THE SPREAD OF *NYŌBŌ-KOTOBA*

In *Amanomokuzu*, it is written that "at court, all food is given a different name. It is bothersome to those who know nothing about this practice. . . . Furthermore, they say that recently, not only all the *nyōbō* but even the women of the Shogun's family are adopting these names."[5] The phrases "all food," "even the women of the Shogun's family," and "all the *nyōbō*" indicate that many foods had been renamed and an increasing number of women used *nyōbō-kotoba* as it spread from the nobility to the samurai class.

Nyōbō-kotoba gradually came into popular use as young women from the lower classes went into service in the homes of the nobility and the daughters of the nobility were married off to feudal lords. It was further spread from the homes of the feudal lords and samurai by daughters of the townsfolk who were employed there. Some were the daughters of poor families who worked as maids, but in the Edo period, it became common for the daughters of wealthy townsfolk to be sent to the estates to learn manners in training for marriage, and they, too, helped spread this style of speech throughout society.

The state of this diffusion is aptly expressed in the *kyōgen* play, *Ohiyashi*. Note that *ohiyashi* was a word used by *nyōbō* to denote "water." The following conversation occurs in the play:

Master:	*Are e ite, o-hiyashi o musunde koi!*
	"Go over there and draw me some *o-hiyashi*."
Servant:	*Nani ga dō ja to ohoseraruru?*
	"What did you say you wanted me to do?"
Master:	*Iya ano taki no o-hiyashi o musunde koi to ifu*[6] *koto ja.*
	"I said, 'Go draw me some *o-hiyashi* from that waterfall.'"
Servant:	*Ano taki no mizu o kunde koi to ohoseraruru koto ka?*
	"Are you telling me to draw you some water from that waterfall?"
Master:	*Naka naka.*
	"That's right. That's what I said."
Servant:	*Mizu naraba mizu kumu de yoi koto o.*
	O-hiyashi o musube to wa . . ., to iute[7] *warafu.*
	"'If you wish me to draw water that is

Master: fine, but what is this *o-hiyashi*?' he says
and laughs."
*Sore wa nanji ga nani mo shiranu ni yotte
ja. Mina uheuhedairikata no jōrōtachi wa,
o-hiyashi o musubu to koso ohoserarete,
mizu wo kumu nado to wa ohoserarenu.
Sochimo ima kara ihinarahe.*
"That's because you don't know
anything. All the refined people at
court all say *o-hiyashi o musubu*, 'to draw
the honorable cooled thing' and don't
say *mizu wo kumu* 'to draw water.'
You use it, too, from now on."

Servant: *Mottomo uheuhe no jōrōtachi ya chigo-wakashūra
wa o-hiyashi tomo musubu to ohoserareyou ga, omae
no yōna ohokina kuchi kara to iute warafu.*
"'Well, the refined people at court, children,
and young people may say *o-hiyashi o musubu*,
but it doesn't suit a mouth as big as yours,
master,' he says and laughs."
(Nonomura 1931, 72 [underlining by Endō])

From this conversation, we can see that *nyōbō-kotoba* has entered the speech of the warrior class. Not only that, it has also begun to be used by men. It is regarded as a tool to raise one's status, but, at the same time, with a kind of disdain. By copying *nyōbō-kotoba*, the fuedal lord is trying to make himself appear refined, but his servant pokes fun at him, pointing out that using refined expressions with "a big mouth like his master's" is nothing more than a thin veneer.

Other examples of men using *nyōbō-kotoba* in *kyōgen* plays are *osanai*, "young," twice being used to mean *kodomo* "children" in *Oni no mamako* (The Demon's Stepchild) and *Konusubito* (The Child Stealer); *kukon* for *sake*, "rice wine," in *Hanako; hamojii* for *hazukashii*, "embarrassing, shameful," in *Uji musubi* (Tying Clans), and *mushi* for *miso*, "bean paste," in *Senjimono* (The Decoction). All of these expressions except *kukon* are used in lines spoken by men.

As is fitting for a didactic work, honorifics are frequently used in *Menoto no sōshi*, an instructional text for women. An elegant and refined lexicon has been chosen for this work, including items from *nyōbō-kotoba*. Examples include *ogushi* for *kami*, "hair," *osanai* for *kodomo*, "children," and *kukon* for *sake*, "rice wine," as well as the verbs *ohiru naru* for *okiru*, "to get up," and *ohirou* for *aruku*, "walk."

As *nyōbō-kotoba* came into popular use, it developed beyond the framework that the ladies of court had originally created and used, as other speakers developed new lexical forms using the same style and methods. For example, the so-called *moji kotoba,* where *sushi* became *sumoji,* was further extended as commoners created new forms.

In the *kyōgen* play entitled *I Moji* (The Character "*I*"), place-names starting with "*i*" such as Iga, Iyo, Inaba, and Ise are represented by the expression *i moji*. Mashimo (1948) reports that in works by Chikamatsu Monzaemon (1653–1724), a playwrite representative of the Edo period, there are fifteen examples of coined words including *isomoji* for <u>isogashii</u>, "busy," *yamoji* for <u>iya</u>, "disagreeable," and *rinmoji* for <u>rinki</u>, "jealous." The word *pā-moji* (from *padre*) was even coined to refer to Roman Catholic priests.

Some expressions came into use among the men of the samurai class as well, a fact lamented in *Kagomimi*: "It is unpleasant to hear samurai, tradesmen, and artisans use words that are women's. Examples such as *onaka* for *hara,* 'belly,' *himojii* for *hidarui,* 'weary,' *kamoji* for *kami,* 'hair,' *otsuke* for *shiru,* 'broth,' *okowa* for *kowameshi,* 'glutinous rice steamed with red beans,' *akanomeshi* for *sekihan,* 'festive red rice,' *yogoshi* for *aemono,* 'dishes dressed with sauces,' *kinako* for *mame no ko,* 'soybean flour' are all too frequently used."[8] There are also examples of men using words such as *murasaki, himojii,* and *okabe* in a collection of popular comic stories called *Seisuishō* (1623).

Ukiyo buro (1812), a work by Shikitei Sanba (1776-1822), contains examples of *nyōbō-kotoba* being used by the daughters of the townsfolk. The following conversation about *moji kotoba* is an excerpt from this work (*NKBT* 1967, 225):

Hatsu: *Hon ni makoto ni kanshin da nee. Watakushidomo wa <u>hitosuji</u> de totonoeta <u>uchimaki o</u> ichido itadaite mo kono mane wa dekimasen.*
        "I really admire her. Even if we ate <u>100</u> portions (a huge amount) of <u>uchimaki</u> 'rice' at one time, we couldn't match her."

Musu: *Oya. Maharikudoi koto o oihi da nō. <u>Hyaku</u> ga <u>kome</u> o ichidoki ni tabete mo to oihi na.*
        "Well, that's a roundabout way of saying things. You should have said, 'Even if we eat one hundred portions of rice at one time.'"

Hatsu: *Oya, o-musu san, ikana kotte mo . . . o, ho, ho, ho, ho. Isso mō kanshin no okosandanē.*
        "Well, O-musu, I just couldn't say that." (Laughs)

Musu: *Watakushi wa nadai no otenba da mono wo. Hai, ochappī to otenba wo ne. Hitoride shotte orimasu. Sore da kara ne, kanshin na oshamoji da yo.*
        "Well, I'm known for my bold, free ways. I'm the only one around like this. So, I'm a regular <u>chatterbox</u>."

O-same: *Oya, oya, '<u>o-shamoji</u>' to wa, '<u>shakushi</u>' no koto de gozaimasu*

> *yo . . . o, ho, ho, ho, ho.*
> "Why! Dear me! '*O-shamoji*' means a '<u>ladle</u>.'" (Laughs)
Musu: *O-same san, honni ka he? Watakushi wa mata oshaberi no*
> *koto ka to omohimashita . . . Sushi o 'sumoji.' Sakana o*
> *'samoji' to oihida kara, oshaberi mo, '<u>o-shamoji</u>'de yoi ga nē?*
> "O-same, is that true? I thought that it meant a talkative
> person. <u>Sushi</u> is called '<u>sumoji</u>' and <u>sakana</u> is called
> '<u>sa</u>moji,' so I thought that <u>o-shaberi</u> would be '<u>o-shamoji</u>.'"

Hatsu and O-same, both of whom have served in trying samurai homes, are to use the refined language they learned there, but Musu reacts negatively to this, saying that language like that "beats around the bush." However, by incorporating one method used to coin expressions in refined women's speech, Musu does coin the word *oshamoji* to denote herself as *oshaberi* (a talkative person). Here we can see both how young townswomen criticize their friends who use refined speech, and how the common people are able to give the language a twist when it suits them.

NOTES

1. McCullough adds the following footnote to her translation, "A play on Hotoke's names, which can mean 'Buddha.'"

2. The "lady" is Shigehira's wife.

3. *Nō, kyōgen jō, chū, ge* (Iwanami bunko, Iwanami shoten, 1990).

4. Unless otherwise stated, all citations of *kyōgen* works are from the collection Ōkura Torahiro (1758–1805) compiled in 1792. Please see, *Ōkura Torahirōbon Nō, kyōgen: Jō, chū, ge* (Iwanami shoten, 1990).

5. *Amanomokuzu.* In *Gunshoruijū 28shū* (Meicho fukyūkai, 1954), pp. 226–27.

6. "To say" is written *iu* in modern Japanese, but in Old Japanese it was written *ifu. Kyōgen shūsei* (Nonomura 1931), the source of these examples, uses both forms, and I have followed its practice.

7. See note 6.

8. *Kagomimi* in *Shinpen kisho fukuseikaisōsho 3* (Rinsen shoten, 1988), pp. 226–27.

CHAPTER 3
WOMEN'S LANGUAGE IN THE EDO PERIOD: REINFORCEMENT OF RESTRICTIONS ON WOMEN'S SPEECH

WOMEN'S LIVES DURING THE EDO PERIOD

From the 17th through the late 18th centuries, Confucian ideologies of male domination over women infiltrated the privileged classes as samurai increasingly pursued the study of Chinese classics. Many books were produced to instruct women on proper behavior, and the so-called weaker, inferior sex was compelled to speak with feminine refinement in a style based on *nyōbō-kotoba*.

It is difficult to establish exactly how women spoke at the beginning of the Edo period. We can make deductions based on conversational passages in written texts, but since these texts include the speech of women from a variety of social classes in a variety of situations, it is difficult to generalize. Let us take the speech of a character from a Chikamatsu Monzaemon work as one example of the language spoken by women at the time.

In the following scene from *Onna goroshi abura no jigoku* (A Woman's Murder, the Hell of Oil), O-kichi, the wife of oil merchant Shichizaemon, admonishes the neighbors' son for spending most of his time in the pleasure quarters.

> *Sadameshi konasama no kokoro ni wa. ... Kosashideta to nikukaro ga. ... kautau na anigo wo tehon ni shite. Akindo to ifu mono wa ichimon zeni mo ada ni sezu. Suzume no su mo kufu ni tamaru, zuibun kaseide oyata-chi no katadasuke to ya. Shingwan tatesanse. Waki he wa ikanu sono mi no shaugon, haa ki ni iranu yara henji ga nai. Ane oja. Hayau mairau. Michi de kochi no hito ni ahashan shitara. Hondō ni matte iru to ifute kudasanse. (NKBT 1958, 394)*

> "In your heart ... it will pain you to hear this as you undoubtedly think it none of my business.... You must take your reliable older brother as an example. Merchants do not waste one coin of money, as they say many drops make a shower, so promise with your heart you will work hard and assist you parents. Acting with virtue is for your own good. Well, since you don't answer you are surely offended. Come, let us leave immediately. If you meet my

husband in the street, <u>please</u> tell him I am waiting in the main building." (Underlining by Endō)

The underlined phrases in this speech of a merchant's wife are honorific forms. For example, in her opening phrase O-kichi addresses her neighbor with *konasama*, literally meaning "the honorable one before me." She also makes use of honorific verb forms, calling her own daughter to leave with the humble verb *mairau* "come/go."

In contrast, her husband speaks to her in plain form:

> *Kore O-kichi. Hito no sewa mo yoi tokoro ni shita ga yoi. Wakai onna*
> *ga wakai otoko no obi toite. Saushite ato de kami de nugufu to wa birō*
> *shigoku, utagahashii. Yoso no koto wa hokarakashite, sā sā mairau hi ga*
> *takeru. (NKBT 1958, 399)*

> "Come on O-kichi, enough meddling in other people's business. It is outrageously impolite for a young woman to unfasten a young man's belt and treat him unkindly afterwards. It's suspicious. Leave other's business alone and come along, now, let's go. The sun is setting."

Shichizaemon only once uses an honorific, the humble verb *mairau*, when he addresses his wife. Note, however, that although the verb takes the same humble form as when O-kichi calls her daughter to leave, in this context it does not have humbling connotations. In Shichizaemon's instance, *mairau* (*mairō*) is a pompous form of the verb *iku* "to go."

Similar use of polite forms by women is found in the fairytale *Urashima Tarō*. In the following passage, Otohime bids farewell to Urashima as he leaves the underwater paradise he has visited.

> Ima wakarenaba, mata itsu no yo ni ka <u>ahi mairase safurahanya</u>.
> Nise no en to mauseba, tatohi kono yo ni te koso yume maboroshi
> no chigiri nite <u>safurafu</u> to mo, kanarazu raise ni te wa, hitotsu ha-
> chisu no en to <u>mumaresase ohashimase</u>. (*NKBT* 1958, 341)

> "Though we part today, I am sure we will <u>meet</u> again. It is said the bond between husband and wife <u>is</u> a bond of the present and the future. In this life, it may be a dream, or an illusive vow not yet exchanged. Please <u>do me the honor of next coming</u> into being on the same lotus as I." (Underlining by Endō)

Otohime uses honorific phrases such as *ahi mairase safurafu*, "will most humbly meet," *hitotsu hachisu no en to mumaresase ohashimase*, "to be most honorably born on the same lotus." Her frequent use of honorifics makes her

41

speech extremely polite. However, not all the women characters in literary texts at the time consistently speak in honorifics. Let us look finally at a scene from Chikamatsu's *Keisei mibu dainenbutsu*, in which a lady of noble birth is speaking harshly to her servant.

> *Ore wa miyako he nobori mita ga, hon ni mibu ni sono mama ja. Sate gwan wo kakeshimono wa men wo kite ganshu ga kyōgen wo suru. Ore ga myōdai ni dare zo kyōgen wo sase yo. (NKBT 1960, 51–52)*

> "I went to the capital and saw for myself that it really is *mibu*. The temple petitioner wore a mask and performed in front of those hearing the requests. Have someone perform for me."

From the above extract it is clear that women of the time used *ore*[1] to refer to themselves. Furthermore, we can see that women did not use honorifics when speaking to their servants.

CONFUCIANISM AND WOMEN'S LIVES

The many books of instruction and manners published during the Edo period are an indication of the rigid control that society exercised over women's speech and behavior. These widely-used texts were considered to be the cornerstone of education for women. The instructions for women written by the esteemed Counselor of the Edo Shogunate, Matsudaira Sadanobu (1758–1829), include one view of woman that is typical of the period:

> All women should be illiterate. A woman with ability encounters large obstacles. They do not need to study anything. Being able to read books written in *kana* is sufficient. Of course, they should never be permitted to train in the martial arts. Women merely spend the day idly at home, so trivial matters are their sphere of knowledge. (Yamakawa 1956, 30)

Instructional etiquette materials were based on the so-called *Onna shisho* (Four Books for Women) of 1656, which was modeled on the text *Shisho* (The Four Books), a set of Confucian writings that was required reading for boys. The name and format of *Onna shisho* indicates the significance for women of the main four books from which it was compiled. These books summarized four Chinese Confucian instructional texts for women: *Onna kōkyō* (Women's Classic of Filial Piety), *Onna rongo* (Analects for Women), *Jokai* (Admonishment to Women), and *Naikun* (Instructions for Women). Similarly, *Kana retsujo den* (Kana Biographies of Famous Women), a translation of a collection of anecdotes about model women in China was also published in 1656.

In addition to these works imported from China, conduct literature appeared combining Buddhist thought and the philosophy of the compilers themselves, a category that includes *Jokunshō* (Book of Precepts for Women, 1642), *Jokunshū* (Collection of Instructions for Women, 1646), *Onna kagami* (A Mirror for Women, 1649), and *Onna shikimoku* (Woman's Formulary, 1649). These works were all lengthy and elaborate in content, geared to the upper classes. However, from the end of the 17th century to the beginning of the 18th, increasing numbers of young women from the lower classes became literate, creating a demand for copybooks for practicing handwriting. Simplified and shortened versions of these Confucian manuals of behavior were adapted and used in new copybooks. Their purpose was to ensure that young girls began internalizing Confucian ideals of behavior at an early age.

Kaibara Ekiken (1630–1714), a Confucian scholar of the Edo period, carried on the teachings of earlier conduct manuals in the texts *Joshi wo oshieru hō* (Principles for the Instruction of Women, 1710) and *Onna daigaku takarabako* (Treasure Chest of Higher Learning for Women, 1716), which were produced as comprehensive etiquette or conduct textbooks for women. *Joshi wo oshieru hō* specifically addresses the education of girls. Here Ekiken states, "Boys mix with their teachers and friends out of doors and learn many things from the world around them. However, because girls are always inside the home and cannot learn from society, their parents must educate them well" (Yūhōdō bunko, ed., 1911, 391).

Ekiken goes on to set down the "Four Conducts," the four things in which women should strive to excel: feminine virtues, feminine language, feminine appearance, and feminine arts and crafts. The basis of his teachings, as he himself states, is the *Jokai* (*OS* 1928) (Admonishments to Women), written by China's Cao Dajia (45–117).

Naikun (Instructions for Women) is another of the Chinese conduct books written for women. Written by empress Renxiao (Wen), wife of emperor Chen zu (Wen) of the Ming dynasty, the third chapter is entitled "Language Discretion," and instructs that care should be taken in language use.

> As the proverb says, if one gently points out another's error, no matter how stubborn the person, you will be listened to. If one speaks ill of another without cause or tells stories, this will spread like wildfire, and one will not be able to stop the damage. One's mouth is like a door; it should be closed when not in use, and needless words should be left unspoken. Words become untrustworthy if they are constantly used. One must be careful with

one's language. In particular, women should speak quietly and with grace. Because nothing good comes of speaking too much, one should keep one's words sparse. (*OS* 1928, 708)

Being raised from infancy to obey and serve others, it is likely that women did not experience the full joy of living. Many of them lamented the fate of being born a woman and lived lives of fatalistic resignation.

LANGUAGE TRAINING IN THE EDO PERIOD

Language use was the object of much comment and instruction in this society where women led such difficult lives, as a look at the conduct books shows. For example, in *Onna dōshi kyō* (Teachings for Women and Children), we find the following passages:

> Women who talk a lot become vulgar, and resemble a courtesan who flatters and flirts.
> Speak quietly when one has something to say. One should not open one's mouth and show one's teeth.
> Once one has said too much it is impossible to stop people's criticism, no matter how much one excuses oneself. (*NKTJY* 1973, 251)

Similarly, in *Joshi wo oshieru hō*, Ekiken devotes several passages to outlining what language women should avoid and how women should be educated. The following segment exemplifies his thoughts.

> Rough words, undignified speech, putting on airs, complaining of one's hatred of others, being proud of one's self, laughing slanderously at others, and acting superior to others are all hideously detestable.
> Do not speak untruths, choose your words, do not speak slanderously of others, speak when necessary, and do not speak otherwise. (Yūhōdō bunko, ed., 1911, 395)

Furthermore, Ekiken warns that chatter can lead to divorce and family chaos.

> The seven grounds for divorce state that if one's wife speaks too much, she can be divorced. If a wife is a chatterbox, and speaks in a vulgar manner, her parents, siblings and relatives will quarrel with each other, and the family will be torn apart. As is written in the old texts, if women speak like men, it will cause disorder in the family. Generally, family strife originates with women, and it is what comes out of women's mouths that causes the trouble. (Yūhōdō bunko, ed., 1911, 398–99)

Finally, here are Ekiken's comments on women's education.

> Make girls learn *kana* from the age of seven, and teach them
> Chinese characters. Also, have them read many classical poems
> that do not include any suggestive ideas. It is good have them ac-
> quire knowledge of the world of *waka*. Also, it is best to teach them
> in the same order as boys are taught by first introducing short
> phrases and sayings. Then, have them read the precepts and ana-
> lects, and Cao Dajia's *Jokai* and so forth, and teach them the way of
> filial obedience and chastity. (Yūhōdō bunko, ed., 1911, 396)

Here, Ekiken states that girls should also be made to learn Chinese and to
read Chinese books. The need for women to have a grounding in Chinese
had been discussed from the Muromachi period; however, women were
still expected to learn the Japanese syllabary first and Chinese characters
second, that is, in the opposite of the order in which boys were taught.
Moreover, women were taught Chinese characters only to allow them to
absorb Confucian thought, not to let them engage in meaningfully construc-
tive analytic or logical thought.

In *Shinsen onna yamato daigaku* (New Selection of Yamato Higher
Learning for Women) edited by Rakuhoku Shōshi in 1785, the code of conduct is extended to dealings with employees and servants and includes the
following advice about language use: "Women should never once use catch-
words or vulgar language. Exercise modesty, because a person's disposition
is made manifest to others through words" (*NKTJY* 1973, 315). He goes on to
state, "Even if servants defy you and speak vulgarly, it is degrading and unseemly to scold them using vulgar language." Subsequent conduct manuals
also instructed women in how they should speak to servants.

LANGUAGE COERCION

Books that elucidated the rules for language use and linguistic conduct for
women with concrete examples from classical texts came to be published
later in the Edo period. *Katakoto* (Faltering Words, 1647), written by the
haiku poet Yasuhara Teishitsu (1610–73), is a book giving instruction about
correct language use, focusing on mistakes in pronunciation, grammar, and
vocabulary that were common at that time.

> It is desirable for children, young men, and women to speak
> in a thin and delicate voice that is as kind, low, and quiet as pos-
> sible. Bookish, overly serious expressions are not becoming. They
> should not use the Chinese-style reading of the characters, but the
> Japanese-style.

> It is not becoming for children, beggars or young women to say *sakujitsu*, "yesterday," and *issakujitsu*, "the day before yesterday," when they should say *kinō* and *ototoi*, or to say *myōnichi*, "tomorrow," and *myōgonichi*, "the day after tomorrow," when they should say *asu* and *asatte*. (Yasuhara 1978, 17)

Yasuhara's appeal for soft and gentle speech echoes the sentiments of earlier writers. However, his call for the use of Japanese expressions over and above Chinese expressions is a new restriction supported by explicit examples. *Fujin yashinaigusa* (hereafter *Yashinaigusa*), a book of etiquette and precepts for women published by Umejima Sanjin in 1689, is composed of five volumes, each having forty to fifty headings. The table of contents includes such items as the origin of words, the history of manners and customs, different names for wives, daughters, mistresses, nuns, matchmakers, and midwives, the history of China, and anecdotes about famous people, but it is mainly a book for the instruction of women. Passage twenty-nine of the fifth volume contains the heading "About how women should mind what they say, and the language used by maids." Umejima states the following:

> People lose interest in a woman who uses rough language like the samurai of the Kanto region, speaks in childish sentence fragments, and makes mistakes in the particles in stories and poems. One's speech reveals one's heart, and it is very important that women take care to be tasteful in their language. Do not say anything that is of no benefit. The more one talks, the more lies will be told.[2]

It is interesting to see that the practice of criticizing women for using masculine language dates back at least to Umejima's time. To counteract this kind of masculine language use, Umejima provides a list of dignified expressions, prefaced with, "Since there is no way for women to live without speaking, I will discuss the matter by category." His lists of expressions are itemized according to types of articles:

Yamato Expressions for Clothing and Accessories

Kosode	"kimono" is called *gofuku*
hara	"belly" is called *o-naka* "honorable middle"
yogi	"bedclothes" is *yoru no mono* "night things"
kaya	"mosquito net" is *kachō*
noru koto	"to ride" is *mesu;*
neru koto	"to sleep" is *o-shizumaru* "honorific + to become quiet."

Staple Foods

kome	"uncooked rice" is *uchimaki*

meshi	"cooked rice, meal" is *kugo*
chimaki	"rice dumpling wrapped in bamboo leaves" is *maki*
mochi	"rice cake" is *kachin,* "hard thing," or *amo.*

Names of Vegetables

nasubi	"eggplant" is *nasu*
sasage	"a type of green bean" is *sasa*
gobo	"burdock root" is *gon*
na	"greens" are *o-ha* "honorific + leaves," etc.

Names of Fish

iwashi is *omura*	(honorific+ first part of word for purple)
tara	"cod" is *yuki no omana,* "fish of the snow"
kazu no ko	"herring roe" is *kazu-kazu*
tako	"octopus" is *ta-moji*

Names of Utensils

kin ichibu,	"one *bu* of gold," is *kin hyappiki,* "one hundred hiki of gold"
ichimon, nimon	"one *mon,* two *mon*" is *hitotsu, futatsu* "one, two"
shakushi	"ladle" is *shamoji*
nabe	"pot" is *kuro* "black" and so on.[3]

Umejima lists 121 such pairs of words, that is to say, he notes 121 words women should use. Although he refers to these words as *Yamato kotoba,* "native Japanese words," they are, in reality, almost identical to *nyōbō kotoba.* However, the following list contains words not found in documents about *nyōbō kotoba* and therefore believed to have been created during the Edo period.

> *oshitashi* for *shōyu* "soy sauce"
> *yawa-yawa* "soft-soft" for *kaimochi* "rice cake"
> *mu-moji* for *mugi* "wheat"
> *tsukiyo* "moonlit night" for *iizushi* "type of sushi"
> *ankachin* for *an mochi* "bean jam covered rice cake"
> *musubi* for *yakimeshi* "roasted rice balls"
> *shihō* "four sides" for *masu* "square wooden measuring cup"
> *kankuro* "tin, black" for *kannabe* "tin pot"
> *hitotsu* "one" for *ippai* "one cupful"

The words listed above may have been invented by people in the Edo period who attempted to imitate the feeling and copy the manner in which *nyōbō-kotoba* were created. It is also important to note that the *Yamato kotoba* written about in this chapter are not identical to what we call *Yamato kotoba* or *wago* in Japanese today, namely, words of native Japanese, as opposed to Chinese or other foreign origin. What the authors of the *Yashinaigusa* and other such manuals are referring to when they write about *Yamato kotoba* are "expressions which, while based on tradition, are understood as being softer than those of Chinese origin and more feminine" (Sugimoto 1985b, 180).

Writings preceding *Yashinaigusa* that discussed *nyōbō-kotoba* explained it as a language used by women serving the imperial court and which differed from the speech of the general populace. However, *Yashinaigusa* also lists the various different names given to women, phrases to be used as ceremonial greetings, and prescribes the language women should use by giving detailed examples.

Kaibara Ekiken and other authors in this genre also give repeated, emphatic, and strict warnings about how language should be used, but none of them get down to lexical specifics and indicate exactly which expressions should be used and when. *Yashinaigusa* does this and more, categorizing words and expressions into groups, organizing rules and restrictions, and generally systematizing women's language. In its day, it was seen as a digest of teachings and a policy guide of language etiquette for women.

Published three years after *Yashinaigusa*, Takai Ranzan's *Onna chōhōki* (Record of Important Matters for Women, 1692) explains in even more detail than *Yashinaigusa* what rules should be observed in regard to language. The following instructions fall under the heading "Regarding women's speech":

> Ordinary women should not be raised near men. Women who grow up among men have minds like them, and their speech resembles that of men. The use of men's language by women is disagreeable to the ears and difficult to understand. Women should speak gently, saying only a word here and there. Speaking and feigning knowledge of words of Chinese origin is exceedingly wrong. To soften all words, *o* and *moji* should be added. (Namura ed. 1981, 21)

Takai sets up men's language and women's language as opposites and strongly warns against women's use of men's language. It is for this reason that Takai emphasizes raising males and females separately from a very young age. Furthermore, he advocates that women speak in a gentle manner using childish and poorly formed expressions, even though this manner of speaking is criticized in *Yashinaigusa*. Similarly, he believes that it is bad for women to sound argumentative and to use expressions of Chinese origin. Moreover, he instructs women to use expressions softened by adding *o* and *moji*, affixes which were characteristic of *nyōbō-kotoba*, thereby illustrating how the language of the *nyōbō* was constructed as the model for women's language in general.

The *Onna chōhōki* continues further, listing examples of *wago* and the corresponding *kango*, and admonishes against use of the latter. Two examples are quoted below.

> It is wrong to say *kerai* "retainer" or *genin* when one should say *uchi no mono* "our person" or *shimo jimo*.
> Saying *naigi* "[somebody's] wife" and *naishitsu* when one should say *okusama* and *ouchi sama* is overwrought. (Namura ed. 1981, 21)

He gives thirteen pairs of *kango* and *wago* synonyms and criticizes each of the *kango* items with thirteen different adjectives. That is to say, using *kango* in speech is "bad, overwrought, ugly, prosaic, pretentious, disagreeable, trite, grating on the ears, mannish, hard as a rock, unpleasant to hear, impatient-sounding, and deplorable." This indicates the strength of his reaction to women's use of words of Chinese origin.

Onna chōhōki continues on to give examples of popular expressions and rough language. It admonishes women not to use them either.

> Good women should not use popular expressions such as *nikui yatsu*, "unpleasant person," *tareme* "who," *suki to* "cleanly, refreshingly," *shika to* "certainly," *hidoi* "terrible," *gebiru* "to become vulgar," *yaku* "to be jealous," *ki no tooru* "considerate," and *oteki* (a second person pronoun used in the pleasure quarters). (Namura ed. 1981, 21)

Next comes a passage entitled "The Soft Speech Used by Women," which gives thirty-four words that were considered "gentle and soft." It states that *kodomo* "children" are to be called *osanai* "young," *naku* "to cry" is *o-mutsukaru*, and *neru* "to sleep" is *o-shizumaru*.

Onna chōhōki also contains a section on *Yamato kotoba*. In it 100 words are divided among the five categories: *kirui* "kinds of clothing," *shokurui* "kinds of staple food," *gyorui* "kinds of fish," *aomono* "vegetables," and *shodōgu* "implements." Most of the words listed are found in *Yashinaigusa*, although some differences are noted such as *konuka* being called *machikane* and *tōkibi mochi* (corn rice cake) being called *morokoshi*. In *Yashinaigusa*, two expressions for *sake* (rice wine), *kukon* and *sasa* are given, whereas in *Onna chōhōki*, only *kukon* appears.

Onna chōhōki strongly denounces the use of words of Chinese origin by women, and admonishes women "not to use one word of slang," of which it gives examples. Words of Chinese origin are believed to sound stronger and harder than words of Japanese origin, besides sounding more theoretical and strongly assertive. It is for these reasons that they were thought unsuitable for women. Slang and popular expressions were strictly forbidden not only because they were vulgar, but because men wanted women to appear untouched by the outside world. In addition to listing taboo words, which it warns should be used with discretion, *Onna chōhōki* gives more precise exhortations than *Yashinaigusa* and increases the number of forbidden words.

Later, in 1712, a similar instructional text entitled *Jochūkotoba* (Women's Language) was printed, and it would be followed by many more such books in the subsequent years. By the beginning of the Meiji period dozens of such texts were in existence. The texts discussed above indicate how severe the control of women's language use became as feudal institutions permeated the society during the Edo period. These texts continuously preach morality in the use of language, tenaciously repeating that a woman's every word should be rephrased in "feminine" speech and that she must speak gently in a manner different from men.

The rules governing the speech of women in the Edo period have been carried over to the present day and still regulate so-called "women's speech." The guidelines for women's language use can be summarized as follows:

> (1) Women should use feminine language;
> (2) Women should use gentle language;
> (3) Women should not use coldly logical words of Chinese origin;
> (4) Women must not use men's language;
> (5) Women should add the honorific prefix *o* and use polite language.

Even now, at the beginning of the 21st century, young women are still occasionally given this kind of advice about their language.

THE LANGUAGE OF THE PLEASURE QUARTERS

The language of the pleasure quarters was created and used by the courtesans and prostitutes of the Yoshiwara, Shimabara, and other such areas in the Edo period. It also influenced subsequent woman's language.

The Edo Shogunate officially sanctioned pleasure quarters in Edo's Yoshiwara, Kyoto's Shimabara, and Osaka's Shinmachi. At the end of the 18th century, upwards of 6,000 prostitutes worked in these districts (Wakita 1987, 128). They were indentured in late childhood or early adolescence for a term of about ten years—longer if they incurred debts—and confined to a quarter of town surrounded by a moat and a high fence. Prostitutes were brought from all parts of the country, so the quarters were a gathering of women who were raised in regions where honorific language was not used and in regions with local dialects. The "quarters dialect" was created to hide regional accents and normalize speech in the quarters. Most of the language that the prostitutes created was honorific, and these expressions were indispensable when dealing with their customers.

Satonamari (Dialect of the Quarters, 1786) records conversations between prostitutes and their samurai customers, such as the following:

Jorō:	*Kinō Mukōjima he ikinshita ga (=ikimashita ga),*
	isso omoshirō arinshita (=arimashita). Wacchi
	(=watashi) isso samurai ni naritō ariisu (=arimasu)
Prostitute:	"Yesterday, I went to Mukōjima. It was amusing. I'd like to be a samurai."
Kyaku:	*Kitsui awaseyō sa.*
Customer:	"That would be difficult!"
Jorō:	*Oya, bakarashii. Honni samurai ni naritakute*
	nariisen (=narimasen).
Prostitute:	"Oh, you're silly! I really mean to become a samurai."
Kyaku (samurai):	*Naze?*
Customer (a samurai):	"Why?"
Jorō:	*Ai sa, samurai wa ne, arimosenu ikusa wo ukeotte*
	chigyō to yara wo totte inansu (=oraremasu) kara sa.
Prostitute:	"Well, because samurai live by the spoils of wars that in fact have not been fought, you know."
	(*KBSJ* 1911, 507 [underlining by Endō])

Also in *Naniwa dora* (Yoshida 1952b, 44) (Gong of Naniwa), written near the end of the 17th century, examples are given of how prostitutes spoke, such as: *Sare kōbe ga mono wo itta koto wa gozansenu* "The skull did not say anything"; *Saa itte misashanse (=osshaimase)* "Well, tell me, please"; and *Mazu are e okaeri asobashimase* "First, go back there." The use of words inflected to create honorifics, *ariisu, ozariisu, gozansu, asobase,* and *osseisu,* for example, is one characteristic of language of the pleasure quarters, which can also be seen in the speech of a geisha in *Sato uguisu* (Warbler in the Quarters), a love story set in Edo and written in 1818.

Nushi ni chitto ne, hanashi ga ozariishite (=gozaimashite), meeriishita (mairimashita) yo.
"I had a little something I wanted to ask you and so I came here."

Nushi no <u>okomari nansu</u> (=okomari ni narareru) koto wo <u>mōshiishitara</u>
(=mōshitara) yomoya oiran mo, iya to wa <u>osseesumee</u> (=osshaimasu-
mai).
"If I said something that bothered you, you wouldn't say you
didn't like me, would you?"
(Murakami 1915, 45–46 [underlining by Endō])

The above clearly shows that the use of inflected forms of a variety of honorific expressions, such as *arinsu, ozariisu, gozansu, asobase,* and *osseisu,* was a notable feature of this language. *Ariisu* and *arinsu* are dialect forms of the verb *arimasu* "exist, have," and their frequent use led to this speech style being called *arinsu kotoba* "*arinsu* language," or *sato namari* "the quarters dialect."

Furthermore, although meanings may have changed in part, several words that are used in modern Japanese had their birth in Edo's pleasure quarters. Examples include words such as *tsū* "connoisseur, authority, expert," *iki* "chic, stylish, tasteful," *yabo* "boor, rustic, someone who isn't knowledgeable of the pleasure district," *mabu* "patron, lover," *iro* "lover of either sex," *ageya* "an establishment to which customers summon prostitutes from the brothels," *chaya* "an establishment that has its own prostitutes and provides food and a place for customers to amuse themselves," *yarite* "madam of a brothel," *zomeku* "to make merry in the pleasure quarters," *ageru* "to call a prostitute to one's room," and *morau* "to call a prostitute who was supposed to have gone to another customer" (Shimada 1971b, 322). These vocabulary items served as an argot that allowed prostitutes to discuss secrets in front of customers.

The use of personal pronouns was also unusual. Where married women of samurai families referred to themselves as *mizukara,* and the wives of wealthy townspeople referred to themselves as *watakushi,* prostitutes called themselves *wacchi* and *oira* and addressed their customers as *nushi* "master." Although the second person pronoun *o-nushi* was used by the upper classes, the honorific *o* was not added to *nushi* in the speech of the prostitutes. Kikuzawa suggests that "all customers were treated the same no matter what their social standing" (Kikuzawa 1940, 273).

The language of the pleasure quarters created a unique mood and feeling that pleased the men who came seeking a world apart from their everyday existence. This fostered the continued development of this distinctive form of speech and its transmission to other areas. After Japan reopened itself to the world during the Meiji period, some of these expressions from the pleasure quarters would be considered appropriate for upper-class women to use.

THE LANGUAGE OF THE COMMON PEOPLE
DURING THE EDO PERIOD

It is conceivable that the conduct manuals existed precisely because many women did not obey society's rules about behavior or speech. For example, the *Onna chōhōki* gives fourteen examples of popular expressions that should not be used by women. However, it is surely because women used these terms that Takai Ranzan took offense and singled them out.

Moreover, even if the daughters of the common people were admonished to speak and behave politely, to express themselves delicately, and to talk in a low voice, there were very few places where they could use this gentle, feminine speech style known as *yamato kotoba*. Young women may have had an opportunity to learn and use the various elements of *yamato kotoba* while serving in a samurai mansion, but it is only natural that they would revert to ordinary speech upon returning to their homes. Besides, not all young women went into domestic service.

It was the women of the upper classes who internalized their training in proper speech and who made a habit of using *yamato kotoba*. Commoners used the same language they always had. This is plainly illustrated in the conversations between young women in the book *Ukiyo buro* (Bathhouse of the Floating World).

Niku:	*Ucchatte okyaagare. Ochappiime. Kondo wa ne,* *O-natsu-san. Ano uta ni seu ne.* (*To a child:*) "Leave me alone, you little brat!" (*To her friend:*) "O-natsu, let's sing that song next!"
Natsu:	*Aa, sore ga yoi yo.* "Yeh, that's a good one!"
Komori:	*O-niku-san, iji no warui koto wo ihinasan na. Sōtee omee wa chiisai mono wo ijimeraa. Minna ga naka wo yoku shite o-asobi.* "O-niku, don't say such mean things! You're always teasing the little kids. Everybody play nice now!"
Haru	*Ai.* "O.K.!"
Niku:	*Irazaru o-sewa da. Kamayaganna. Mekusaremee.* "Mind your own business! Leave me alone, you rheumy-eyed bat!"

It should be noted that Niku's speech is almost identical to that which a man would use.

In the following conversation between a mother and daughter and an elderly woman, we can again see the use of rough language that is quite far removed from what was taught as polite speech to women.

Beso:	*Kaka-san, O-bin-san to O-mage-san ga buttaa.*
	"Mom, O-bin and O-made hit me."
Haha:	*Nan da. Kono gakimee. Mata hoete ushaagatta ka.*
	Mitaku demo nee. Do, do, doitsu ga butta.... Unu
	mo mata unu da wa.
	"What? You brats! Scream and run away, will you? Well, I don't want to see your faces again! Who did it?....Well, you're a fine one, too, you know!"
Baba:	*Nan da. Kono kamisan wa. Oyamera, oyamera to*
	kuchigitanee.... Kore, narikonde yokerya, kocchi kara
	narikomu no da yo.
	"Hey! Who do you think you are? Calling their parents rotten, bad-mouthing them?...Well, I'll add my two cents worth if you don't watch out!"
Haha:	*Kore, kore, yakamashii. Chitto damaru ga ii wa na.*
	Toshiyori no kuse ni deshabariyagatte kara ni ....
	"Hey! Hey! Be quiet! You had better shut up! What's an old woman like you putting your nose in where it doesn't belong, anyhow!..."

In *Ukiyo buro*, many different women appear, all using language appropriate to their characters. In addition to the coarse examples above, we also find the following example of the polite language used on the estates:

Yome:	*O-abanō gozaimasu yo. O-shizuka ni asobashimashi.*
	Yasu ka. Dōzo no, koko e o-hiya wo sukoshi o-kure.
	Saasaa, chōdo yō gozaimasu. Omae-san, kore wo o-
	abi asubashite o-agari asubase.
	"That's dangerous! Please settle down! Yasu, bring me a little cold water, please. There, it's just right. Now please rinse yourself with this and get out of the bath."

The author of *Ukiyo buro* adds the note: "This young wife has still not lost her habit of using the speech of the samurai mansions."

Passages in which housewives talk to each other using polite speech are also found in the work:

Mi:	*Saki sama wa o-shūtogo ga gozaimasu ka?*
	"Is her mother-in-law still alive?"
Tatsu:	*Hai, mada wakajūto de gozaimasu.*
	"Yes, and she's young."
Mi:	*Sore wa ano o-kosan o-hone ga oremashō.*
	"Well, it must be difficult for your daughter."

However, Tatsu uses coarse language like the following to those of her household:

Nanda O-uma ka. Nani shi ni kita. Oi, ima, iku yo.
"What? You, O-uma! What did you come for? Yeh, I'm coming now, all right?"

In a love story set in Edo called *Shunshoku yuki no ume* (Spring Views, a Plum Tree in Snow), written by Kyōgentei Shunga (1838), the following conversation unfolds:

O-mine:	*Yaresa, kore de takusan da wa ne.*
	"Well, I'm full now."
Tsunakichi:	*Shako no nita no wa dō dae.*
	"How about some braised squilla?"
Ranchou:	*Mu, soitsu wa yan ya da na.*
	"Well, I don't mind if I do!"
O-mine:	*Aresa, makoto ni omae-san wa iji ga kitanai yo."*
	"Well, aren't you really greedy!"
Ranchō:	*Hoi, ooshikujiri da.Hen, temee no yō ni enryō wo shiishii kūmono yori wa, enryō mo nanimo shinee de kūhō ga tsumi ga nakutte kawaii wa.*
	"You don't know how wrong you are! Eating without any hesitation isn't a crime. And it's much more endearing than your hemming and hawing!"
Tsunakichi:	*Are maa, mō sukoshi ii ja nai ka.*
	"Ah, well, how about some more?" (Murakami ed. 1915, 168)

We may say that the speech of the general populace was not the same as that taught in books on manners and etiquette. In every period, the everyday experiences of, and language used by, commoners had differed from those of the upper classes. So, too, have there been social classes that accepted and emphasized the teaching of manners and those that were far removed from this practice. These two different forms of speech converged in modern society after the Meiji Restoration.

55

NOTES

1. In contemporary Japanese, *ore* is most frequently described as a casual first person pronoun used by men.

2. Umejima Yauemon, *Fujin yashinaigusa*, Wasōbon (Japanese bound edition) (Genroku 2 [1690]), chapters 5–29.

3. Ibid.

CHAPTER 4
WOMEN'S LANGUAGE IN THE MEIJI AND TAISHŌ PERIODS: THE ENTRENCHMENT OF WOMEN'S LANGUAGE IN EDUCATION

In this chapter, I discuss issues of women and language in the period from the Meiji Restoration (1868) through the Taishō period (1912–26), focusing on educational policies. This period saw the introduction of ideas of human rights and gender equality and their suppression under the national ideology of "a wealthy nation and a strong military" and militaristic nationalism, which resulted in gender segregation in education and language use. The ideology of "the good wife and wise mother" and women's language were forced upon women by the patriarchal system, which was itself a microcosm of the imperial government.

THE WOMAN'S LIBERATION MOVEMENT IN THE MEIJI PERIOD

The Meiji Restoration, when the Edo shogunate returned executive powers to the emperor, led to a transformation of the nation's social structure. Discrimination according to traditional social class was abolished, and a new class system was effectively established. A national educational system was set up. Ideas of human rights were introduced from the West and were widely promulgated by intellectuals such as Fukuzawa Yukichi. In his 1874 work, *Gakumon no susume* (The Encouragement of Learning), he criticized misogynistic conduct manuals such as *Onna daigaku*, writing "men are human beings, and women, too, are human beings."

A democratic movement had emerged in the last days of the Tokugawa shogunate, centered on Itagaki Taisuke, who had played a leading role in the overthrow of the shogunate and promoted the modernization of Japan. This movement held public meetings around the country, demanding greater rights and freedoms and popular participation in government. At the movement's peak in 1882, Kishida Toshiko (1863–1901) joined it as an advocate of freedom for women. Kageyama Hideko (later Fukuda Hideko) (1867–1912), moved by one of Kishida's speeches, began holding discussion meetings where she advocated the expansion of women's rights. However, the growth of the democratic movement attracted unwelcome attention from the police, and as the movement shifted its focus to the problem of unequal treaties, both Kishida and Fukuda broke with it.

In 1885, Iwamoto Yoshiharu (1863–1942) established the Meiji School for Women as a Christian-oriented school, and began publishing *Jogaku zasshi* (Journal of Women's Education) the same year. Iwamoto used the school and the magazine as media for advocating the ideal of the equality of men and women as an extension of the equality of all people before God. He also advocated equality between men and women within the family.

Jogaku zasshi was the successor to *Jogaku shinshi* (New Journal of Women's Education), which had been forced out of print. Iwamoto took over *Jogaku shinshi's* goal of raising women who would become "the mothers of geniuses and heroes" (*Jogaku shinshi* 1986, 2). In the first volume of *Jogaku zasshi*, he detailed the purpose of the publication:

> Devoting ourselves to the betterment of women, our modest aspiration is to imitate the West perfectly and to blend Western woman's rights with the traditional feminine virtues of our country. (*Jogaku zasshi* 1984, 3)

Following the tradition of civil rights theorists, in *Yo no fujo tachi ni susumu* (Counsel for the Women of the World, 1886), Ueki Emori (1857–92) states that both males and females have their own individual personalities and advocates education and women's rights, among other progressive ideas. Ueki goes beyond Fukuzawa's and Iwamoto's doctrine of women as "good wives and wise mothers" in viewing women as beings with latent potential who should be active in society. He was at the leading edge of feminist theory at that time (Hirota 1982, 28–29), but this theory was unable to make any progress in the face of the social forces that were gradually making Japan a modern militaristic nation.

As Igeta describes the imperial constitution of 1889, it had the effect of making the "sacred and inviolable" emperor sovereign, barred females from acceding to the imperial throne, gave emperors the right to have concubines and name the sons of these concubines as heirs, and denied suffrage and citizenship to women, whether or not they held property (Igeta 1982, 46). In essence, this constitution codified male dominance and repressed the rights of women.

The Imperial Rescript on Education was issued in 1890. It made the nation's schools the means by which the spirit of the absolutist imperial system was to be inculcated into every family. Children in the upper elementary grades were required to memorize the Imperial Rescript, and school principals read it aloud at school events.

Matsuoka Shizue, who was schooled under this imperial absolutist system, attested to the success of this indoctrination when she made the following remark about the death of the Meiji Emperor on the NHK radio program *Joshi kyōiku shi* (A History of Women's Education; first broadcast in October 1957, and rebroadcast in April 3–6, 1995 on radio channel 1, *Radio Shin'yabin* [discussed later in the book]): "Everyone wanted the Meiji Emperor to live forever, and when he passed away, we were truly overwhelmed with sorrow" (*NHK* April 5, 1995).

WOMEN'S EDUCATION IN THE MEIJI PERIOD

We will now look in detail at the educational policies of the Meiji era. In 1872, the Meiji government expanded the educational system, making schooling compulsory with the following declaration:

> It is recorded that, from this day forth, ordinary people may engage in study on an equal basis. Young children, male or female without exception, must attend elementary school, and the parents of those who do not will be censured. (Masubuchi ed. 1981, 16)

At this time, a system of elementary, secondary, and higher education was established. All schools charged monthly tuition fees, which ranged from 1/10 to twice the amount of a young instructor's monthly salary of four or five yen.[1] Only 39.9 percent of boys and 15.1 percent of girls, a combined average of 28.1 percent of all children, attended school during the following year because of these fees. Women who grew up during that era tell of their parents believing that girls needed little or no schooling.

At the Education Ordinance in 1879, a decision was made to open normal and technical schools for the first time, and the system of gender-segregated education was institutionalized with the words:

> It is forbidden for males and females to be in the same place of learning, although at elementary level there is nothing to prevent this (Article 42). (Masubuchi ed. 1981, 28)

As a result of this ordinance, female students who had been studying at coeducational middle schools under the old educational system were forced to switch to regular and normal schools for girls.

The compulsory subjects in the elementary schools were reading, orthography, calligraphy, arithmetic, and moral training, with the addition of handicrafts or needlework for girls. According to Tanaka, "Education at the time of the expansion of the educational system was linked to the general societal drive to 'Westernize' and the individualism and practicality of the West's educational philosophy was reflected therein. However, the Education Ordinance and the 'Reformed Education Ordinance' issued the following year focused on Confucian thought as the conservatives attempted to place moral and behavioral education in a central position" (Tanaka ed. 1987, 226). Consequently, coeducation was replaced by gender segregation and disparities in educational opportunities and differences in educational content for males and females were institutionalized.

Christian girls' schools had already existed before the national education system was established. *Felice waei jogakkō* (Felice Bilingual Girls' School) was established in 1870, and *Kyōritsu jogakkō* (Cooperative Girls' School) was established in 1871. Other Christian girls' schools, many of which still exist, were established throughout the 1870s. The instructors were Western missionaries who addressed women's education from a humanistic Christian standpoint and young Japanese with new ideas about improving the status of women. However, the speech and behavior of the students, who sometimes naively, and often articulately, discussed these teachings, became objects for social criticism and censure and sensational reports in the press (Hirota 1982, 28). Some parents, even those of high economic and social status, saw such schools as detrimental and would not allow their daughters to attend, maintaining that girls learned nothing there but impudence.

Yet by 1899, women's higher education was well under way. As the government's promotion of education as a means of fostering "good wives and wise mothers" put parents at ease, they became more willing to send their daughters to school. This led to an increase in the number of schools and higher enrollment (Kaihara 1996, 32). In the first years of public education, only 15 percent of girls had been enrolled in elementary schools, not even half of the number for boys, but as the years passed, the gap between the sexes decreased.

Table 3. Percentage change in enrollment (Joseishi sōgō kenkyūkai ed. 1990, 67)

	Total	Boys	Girls
1873	28.13	39.90	15.14
1880	41.06	58.72	21.91
1890	48.93	65.14	31.13
1900	81.48	90.35	71.73
1910	98.14	98.83	97.38

The moral education texts of the era provide a glimpse of the aims and policies of girls' education. In 1883, the Ministry of Education designated *Shōgaku sahō sho* (Elementary Book of Etiquette) as the morals manual for teachers. It contains the following passage: "Boys should be as energetic in their activities as possible, and girls should be as gentle as possible. This distinction extends even into playtime activities" (*Shōgaku sahō sho* in *NKTKS* 1962, 193). It was believed that boys and girls should not only be educated differently from infancy in order to enhance their respective traits of "courageousness" and "gentleness" but that their play should also be segregated.

Shōgaku shūshin sho (Elementary Book of Moral Training), published by the Ministry of Education that same year, was compiled from old proverbs, classical literature, Confucian treatises, and the works of such commentators as Kaibara Ekiken. One text urges girls to study hard, not for their own advancement, but to reflect well on their parents (*Shōgaku shūshin sho* in *NKTKS* 1962, 391). Elsewhere, it advocates the primacy of the husband and the supporting role of the wife (*Shōgaku shūshin kun* in *NKTKS* 1962, 392). Another text outlines the obligations of a meek and dutiful daughter-in-law (*Jinjō shōgaku shūshin sho* in *NKTKS* 1962, 520). It also cites Kaibara Ekiken on the role of the wife in maintaining the quality of life in a household. A textbook published in 1900 echoes the philosophy of the *Onna shisho* in urging women to be "gentle and graceful in all things . . . not only in manners, but also in speech" (*Shinpen shūshin kyōten* in *NKTKS* 1962, 650). Although a 1903 text states, "it is wrong to think that women are inferior to men" (*Jinjō shōgaku shūshin sho* in *NKTKS* 1962, 35), the emphasis elsewhere is on men as masters and women as their helpers. The lip service to female equality may be the result of increased contact with foreign cultures, but the tone of these manuals as a whole reinforces the traditional norms. Even as Meiji Japan moves toward modernization, the ideology of female education laid out in *Onna daigaku* is alive and well.

WOMEN'S LIVES AS ADVOCATED BY WOMEN'S MAGAZINES

Many women's magazines were published in the 1880s. Shut away in the home with limited educational opportunities, women who were hungering for knowledge could not get enough of these magazines. Matsuoka Hisako speaks of the joy of coming across *Jogaku zasshi* (Journal of Women's Education): "What most expanded my views, that is to say, what opened my eyes to reading was *Jogaku zasshi*. I always looked forward to library hour and always got a hold of it to read" (*Joshi kyōiku shi*, NHK Radio).

Magazines from this era can be classified broadly into two types. One held up the ideal of the chaste, good wife and wise mother, and the other pressed for the expansion of women's rights and women's liberation.

In its statement of purpose, *Nihon no jogaku* (Japanese Women's Learning, 1887, Nihon Jogakusha) acknowledged the benefits that could come from women following the same educational and artistic pursuits as men, but advised readers against discarding traditional Japanese "feminine virtues" in the process and advocated women's education mostly for its beneficial effect on home life (*Nihon no jogaku* in FNF1 1986, 3).

On the other hand, some magazines expounded the expansion of women's rights and women's liberation. In its statement of purpose, *Joken* (Women's Rights), contrasted the current subjugation of women with the original state of nature in which "ying and yang were mutually dependent" (*Joken* in FNF1 1986, 2), and it deplored women's lack of economic and political freedom. However, this magazine did not last very long and calls advocating the expansion of women's rights were soon swallowed up by the roar of voices promoting education to produce "good wives and wise mothers."

The more conservative women's magazines justified their calls for gender-appropriate education by voicing fears that "the virtues of chastity, absolute fidelity, elegance, and gentleness, the characteristics of Japanese women that have shown throughout history" (*Jokan* in FNF1 1986, 2) were in danger of disappearing. Many writers during the Meiji period thus fervently advocated not only the continuation of the customs and manners passed down from the Edo period, but also the repudiation of ideas about sexual equality introduced from the West.

These magazines often carried articles about language in the course of describing their ideal image of gentle and graceful women. The "Arts and Sciences" column of volume one of *Fujin kyōiku zasshi* (Journal of Women's Education, 1888) discusses writing under the heading "Use of kana, 1.2." The article states, "Women should make efforts to do all their writing in a simple, gentle hand and should always practice using *kana*" (*Fujin kyōiku zasshi* in FNF1 1986, 21). In advocating the use of *kana*, we see a continuation of the restrictions on women's orthography that had prevailed since the Heian period.

In a similar vein, Volume 221 of *Jogaku zasshi* (1890) carries an article entitled "Woman's Language Usage."

> The language of women is generally elegant . . . and their delicate pronunciation and polite tone cannot be matched by men. However, it seems that rough, impolite, offensive, and ugly-sounding words have entered women's vocabularies recently. . . . In addition, certain women use difficult words of Chinese origin, often with English thrown in, so that their relatives in the country-

side have trouble understanding what they are saying.

It is not so distracting when women speak with men, because they then exercise restraint. However, when women gather and talk among themselves, they seem to use words that are not at all praiseworthy:

Oya anata yoku <u>kita</u> no nee.	"Gee, I'm glad you came."
Watashi no <u>okkasan</u> ga.	"My mom . . ."
Ara iya yo.	"Oh, no!"
Yoku<u>tte yo.</u>	"It's all right."
Naninani <u>da wa</u>.	"It's . . . you know."
Sanpo ni <u>iku</u>?	"Want to go for a walk?"
Kimi wa	"You... "(very familiar form usually used by men)
Boku wa . . .	"I..." (very informal form usually used by men)
Naninani subeshi <u>da yo.</u>	"You should do. . . ."
<u>Ara mā, hontō?</u>	("Oh, dear! Really?")

I doubt that one can maintain a noble and elegant character with words like these. (Underlining by Iwamoto)

The author of this passage is the same Iwamoto who established a girls' school in order to improve women's status in society and who published a magazine to expound these ideas. However, when it came to speech, he was in favor of women using elegant, beautiful expressions, and he could not accept the novel expressions that arose out of the impassioned, fresh new ideas of the female students. Expressions that he was not used to hearing were "bad" expressions, and he was not in favor of women using difficult words of Chinese origin.[2]

Volume 43 of *Tōkyō fujin kyōfūkai zasshi* (Journal of the Tokyo Women's Moral Reform Society, 1891) also contains passages regarding the speech of female students. The magazine proclaims, "Recently, the language of female students speech is tending toward the obscene" and admonishes, "Whether this usage is corrected or not depends on the virtuous character of the woman instructors."

To anyone who has heard present-day Japanese adults criticize the speech of students and young girls as "rough and impolite," these criticisms from over a hundred years ago sound very familiar. In any period of history, men seem to find women's innovations in language difficult to accept.

The plain, nonpolite elements that Iwamoto deplored, such as *yokutte yo* and *da wa* were given the name *teyodawa kotoba*. These were the catch phrases of the language of women in the Meiji period. For example, in an essay published in 1888 titled "Popular Expressions," Ozaki Kōyō listed sentence patterns that elementary school girls had used eight to ten years previously:

> *Ume wa mada sakanakutte yo.*
> "The plum blossoms haven't bloomed yet, you know!"
> *Ara, mō saita no yo.*
> "Oh! Now they have bloomed, you know!"
> *Ara mō saite yo.*
> "Oh! Now they have bloomed, you know!"
> *Sakura no hana wa mada sakanai n da wa*
> "The cherry blossoms haven't bloomed yet."

Ozaki concluded that all the students at girls' schools now talked like this.

The same usage was explained in Volume 25 of *Kijo no tomo* (Ladies' Friend, 1888):

> At the time of the old shogunate, the daughters of samurai of humble means who lived in Aoyama were apt to use these phrases. It shows how language forms can regain popularity, just as smoldering ashes can reignite. If language is elegant, ladies may use it without hesitation, whatever its origin. Poets may use it, too. It is not the humble origins of this language that I criticize, but its countrified air. Thoughtful ladies should not have anything to do with using this language. It would be like polishing a flaw into a beautiful jewel or making a mirror cloudy.
> (*Kōyō zenshū*, vol. 10, 1993, 4–5)

Tayodawa kotoba was also discussed in the newspapers of the day. The September 8, 1891 edition of the *Yomiuri Shinbun* contains an article called "The Bad Habits of Female Students—No. 3," which mentions language: "Conversations between friends have become extremely rough. Straight-laced old women might scowl just to hear people say *sō ne* 'yes, I know,' or *ara yokutte yo* 'my, that's all right.'"

This is only one of many articles that gives *yokutte yo* as an example of bad speech habits. For example, the February issue of *Waseda bungaku* (Waseda Literature, 1895) contains the following remark:

> *Ara yokutte yo* and similar expressions that were once part of the idiom of the outskirts of Ushigome now sound oddly like the speech of young women of the middle and upper classes. . . . These expressions are thought to have first been spread to the mansions in this neighborhood by the lower classes of society. Since these families are prosperous, well-to-do and influential today, may these expressions eventually be transmitted back to the Shitamachi, the low-lying areas where the lower classes live?

From this we learn that expressions like *yokutte yo* had already become commonplace in the speech of middle class women.

Ozaki Kōyō, quoted above as deploring the use of *yokutte yo* and other such expressions, in fact uses them liberally in conversations between young women in her story *Konjiki yasha* (1897).

Toshi: *Yokutte yo, yokutte yo, kore kara mō yokutte yo. (Ozaki Kōyō shū* 1971, 60)
"All right, all right, all right already."

Miya: *Sō ne, da keredo, minna ga ano hito o me no kataki ni shite ranbō suru no de ki no doku datta wa. Tonari atte ita mon da kara watashi made hidoi me ni awasarete yo. (Ozaki Kōyō shū* 1971, 66)
"All right, but everyone seemed to hate the sight of him and was being rude, so I sympathized with him. And just because I was beside her, they gave me a bad time, too."

Miya: *Watashi wa iya da wa. (Ozaki Kōyō shū* 1971, 67)
"I can't stand it."

With continuous use over time despite criticism and censure, *teyodawa kotoba* was finally recognized as the language of women of the middle and upper classes.

Some commentators were of the opinion that while women were loquacious in private, they could not converse properly in public. In Volume 1 of *Fujinkai* (Women's World) published in 1902, Yokoi Tokio writes:

> The women of our country are very eloquent and talkative at gatherings with other women, but much of what they discuss is gossip about other people. Otherwise, they do no more than impulsively spill out the feelings of melancholy that they ordinarily keep to themselves.
>
> On the other hand, when they are at gatherings with men, women do not say a word except to respond to men with a simple "yes" or "no". Geisha are very skilled in verbal interaction and they attempt conversation with men without inhibition or stammering. Since most women are not skilled conversationalists, their precious husbands, fathers, and brothers are attracted to prostitutes. . . . I think it will be important for women of the future to work hard at acquiring the conversational skills that will bridge the gap between men and women. (*Fujinkai* in FNF3 1986, 204)

Even in the Meiji era, as the previously quoted passage from *Jogaku shinshi* shows, women's talkativeness was considered undesirable, just as it had been grounds for divorce in the Edo period. As a result, women felt unable to speak articulately, except in private conversations among themselves.

Meiji women were in a double bind: criticized both for talkativeness and for poor conversational skills that drove husbands and male relatives to prostitutes who were skilled conversationalists. We have to assume that this kind of sophistry was used to justify husbands' associations with geisha and other extramarital relationships.

The first volume of *Fujin kurabu* (The Women's Club), published in 1908 (Shimeisha), carries a piece by Tōgō Masatake titled "Men's Complaints." Here, too, we find criticism of women's conversational skills, but Tōgō goes beyond advocating conversational skills to blaming women for their husbands' neglect.

> This is the most important matter in relating to one's husband and parents-in-law. For example, if a husband talks about various subjects or tells his wife his own thoughts, she must make comments and ask him questions. If she does not do this, her husband will eventually stop speaking to her due to her lack of response. It is a wife's fault if her husband stops having conversations with her. (*Fujin kurabu* in *FNF3* 1986, 15–18)

Women's speech is demeaned as empty of content and inarticulate. As the following excerpt of a young women's speech from *Joshi kyōiku shi* (on NHK Radio) shows, some women were indeed unskilled speakers. The section quoted here is difficult to follow, since the topic is not developed logically.

> Since my mother had passed away, my grandfather in our town, well an unusually stylish young lady, that lady, and , ahhhh, my father, and because there were three of us children, all girls you know, yes, well, please educate them, that sort of thing. . . .

The speech style used here is elegant and polite, but the lack of obvious connections among the sentence fragments could be irritating to a listener. I assume that the speaker was trying to say something like, "Since my mother had passed away and there were three daughters to bring up, my grandfather introduced an unusually stylish young lady to my father as a possible second wife." It is unreasonable to expect a wellborn young woman, who has been continuously trained to think that being logical is unbecoming, to suddenly speak clearly and concisely.

In 1906, the first issue of *Fujin sekai* carried an article in which male opinion leaders responded to the topic "The Virtues of Japanese Women." Ōkuma Shigenobu, a count and founder of Waseda University, wrote as follows:

> We may say that the special qualities of Japanese women are obedience, warmth, and goodness. They do not cling, and have the

ability to take on the good qualities of others. Western women have improved their intellects, and as a result, their social status has risen. However, this has made them arrogant and vain, and many of them are mannish. Their husbands have to put up with the "crowing hens." (*Fujin sekai* in *FNF3* 1986, 14)

In the same feature, the president of Japan Women's College, Naruse Jinzō, lists the following as virtues: "Their virtues include an obedient and patriotic spirit that comes from controlling one's self, subjugating one's self, and sacrificing one's self." The vice-director of the Ministry of Education Bureau of Normal School Affairs, Sawayanagi Masatarō states, "Japanese women are far superior to the women of any other country in the world in practicing the virtue of obedience."

Author Kōda Rohan also writes, "A demure nature and skillful emotional control are the virtues of Japanese women." The president of the Tokyo Metropolitan Women's Teacher's School, Hayashi Goichi, praises "being demure in all things, diffident, and modest." All of the critics praise obedience, demureness, and self-control, the qualities emphasized in girls' education continuously since the publication of *Onna daigaku.*

In an attempt to escape their long-standing oppression, a group of women writers, critics, and artists formed the society known as *Seitō* (Bluestocking) in 1911, and their magazine of the same name served as their medium of expression.

Hiratsuka Raichō, a key figure in this group, made the following declaration in the first issue of the magazine, "In the beginning, woman was the sun, an authentic person. Now, she is the moon, a sickly pale-faced moon, living off others, shining by their light" (Hiratsuka 1911).

Seitō introduced many new works of literature to its readers, stimulating, influencing, and giving courage to women in Japanese society. However, even the women involved in the magazine seemed unaware that feminine language had been a tool of oppression and that the type of language training offered in the schools had produced obedient, restrained women. In fact, when Hiratsuka Raichō was interviewed on the radio program *Joshi kyōiku shi,* she spoke in a much gentler and more refined style than most of the other thirty participants.

In any case, the recent victories over Russia and China had set Japan on a more militaristic course, and *Seitō* came to be seen as dangerously provocative, to the extent that its activities were restricted.

THE LANGUAGE OF MEIJI WOMEN

It is not easy to obtain materials that offer direct evidence for the speech of

Meiji women, so I have used conversations from novels written during that period. I have chosen some dialogues between men and women in order to highlight the differences between male and female speech.

The first example comes from Tsubouchi Shōyō's *Tōseishoseikatagi*. Published in 1885, the thirteenth story contains the following conversation between a university student and a geisha whom he had previously promised to marry:

<blockquote>

Geisha: *Watashi wa ano toki no koto wo omofu to, makoto ni kuyashikute narimasen yo.*
"I get so upset when I think of what happened!"

Student: *Dandan no omae no shinjitsu, kesshite orosoka ni wa omohanai ga, omae mo ima ichido ki wo shizumete yokku atosaki wo kangahete goran.*
"I don't doubt your sincerity, but just calm down and think about your future."

Geisha: *Iie, sonna nigeguchi wa kikimasen . . . Jūnen de mo, nijū nen de mo matte orimasu mono wo.*
"No, I'm not going to listen to your attempt to wriggle out of it. I'll wait for you, even if it takes ten or twenty years."

Student: *Omae mo ammari wakaran jaa nai ka. . . . Mō orea kaeru yo*
"You're probably not sure what you want to do yourself. . . . I'm going home now."
(*Tsubouchi Shōyō shū* 1966, 123–25)

</blockquote>

While the woman adds the polite -*mas*u suffix to verbs and the polite *desu* copula, and uses humble forms such as *matte orimasu*, lit., "(I) will be (most humbly) waiting," the man does not use honorific forms except for one instance of *kangaete goran* "think about it," which is not at the highest level of formality, and he chooses *ore*, the coarsest way to say "I." For "you," he uses *omae*, which indicates both familiarity and the superior position of the speaker. The idea of male superiority is clearly manifest in language use.

Next let us look at the conversation between Takeo and Namiko in Tokutomi Roka's *Hototogisu* (The Cuckoo, 1898):

<blockquote>

Namiko: *Anata, o-tsukare asobashita deshō.*
"You must be tired, dear."

Takeo: *Nami-san koso kutabiretarō. Oh kirei, jitsu ni rippa da. . . . Hontō ni Nami-san ga kō kimono wo kahete iru to, mada kinō kita hanayome no yō ni omofu yo.*
"Nami-san, it is you who must be tired. You look beautiful, really splendid . . . Nami-san, when you wear a kimono like this, it makes me

</blockquote>

Namiko:

Takeo:

Namiko:

feel like you are still my young bride who came only yesterday."

Anna koto wo. . . . Sonna koto wo ossharu
to itte shimahimasu kara.
"Saying such a thing. . . . If you say that, I'm going to end up leaving."

Ha ha ha ha. Mō iwanai. Iwanai. Sō nigen de mo iija
nai ka.
"Ha, ha, ha, ha! I won't say it again. I won't. But you don't have to run away like that, do you?"

Ho ho ho. Chotto kigahe wo itashite mairimasu yo
"Ho, ho, ho! I'm going to go and get changed."

(Tokutomi 1966, 34–35)

Here we see that Namiko uses highly elegant honorifics such as *O-tsukare asobasu*, "be tired," *ossharu*, "say," and expressions of extreme humbleness such as *kigae wo itashite mairu*, "go and get changed." In response, her husband Takeo uses *Nami-san*, which is an honorific title, but other than that he speaks to her in plain language such as, *kutabiretarō*, "you're probably dead tired," *omofu yo*, "(I) think," and *ja nai ka*, "isn't it?"

In another example, a conversation between a man and wife in Natsume Sōseki's *Wagahai wa neko de aru* (I Am a Cat, 1906–7) goes like this:

Wife:

Husband:

Wife:

Husband:

Wife:

Husband:

Wife:

Sen datte chū wa taihen ni yoku kiku kiku to
osshatte mainichi mainichi agatta ja arimasen ka.
"Before, you said that it was very effective and were taking it every day, weren't you?"

Kono aida uchi wa kiita no da yo. Kono goro wa
kikanai no da yo.
"Before, it was working. These days it isn't."

Kongetsu wa chitto tarimasen ga.
"We're a little short this month."

Tarin hazu wa nai. Isha e mo yakurei wa sumashita
shi, honya e mo sengetsu haratta ja nai ka
"There is no way we should be short. We paid the doctor for the medicine, and didn't we pay the bookstore last month?"

Sore de mo anata ga gohan meshiagarande pan wo
o-tabe ni nari, jamu wo o-name ni naru mono desu
kara.
"But we are because you don't eat rice, but eat bread and jam."

Ganrai jamu wo ikukan nameta no kai.
"Exactly, how many cans of jam did I eat?"

Kongetsu wa yattsu irimashita yo.
"Last month I bought eight."

Husband:	*Yattsu? Sonna ni nameta oboe wa nai.*
	"Eight? I don't remember eating that much."
Wife:	*Anata bakari ja arimasen. Kodomo mo namemasu*
	"It's not just you. The children eat it, too."
	(Sōseki zenshū 1965, 30)

While the wife uses honorifics such as *ossharu*, "speak," *agaru*, "take medicine," *meshiagaru* and *o-tabe ni naru*, "eat," *o-name ni naru*, "taste" to her husband and deals with him using the polite verb endings *desu* and *-masu*, her husband does not use any honorific expressions, only plain sentence endings such as . . . *da yo*, . . . *ja nai k*a (interrogative), and . . . *kai* (interrogative).

The level of honorifics used by the women varies somewhat, but there is no denying the fact that they all express themselves using honorifics when speaking about the actions of their male counterparts. On the other hand, even when women use honorifics and polite endings towards men, men do not use honorifics in return, but converse in plain forms. The consistent use of plain form sentence endings seems like an expression of male feelings of superiority. Comparing these Meiji works to *Ukiyo buro* and other Edo-period works in which there are few gender differences in the language of the common people, we can see how entrenched these distinctions were in the language of the Meiji period.

Now, let us take a look at how women spoke among themselves. For five nights beginning on October 14, 1957, Japan's national radio network NHK broadcast a series called *Joshi kyōiku shi*, "A History of Women's Education," in which thirty-four women and four men born in the Meiji period or earlier spoke of their experiences in education during the early years of Meiji. The program was rebroadcast in April 1985 as part of the celebration of NHK's 75th anniversary (April 3–6, radio channel 1, *Rajio shinyabin)*. These personal accounts by living witnesses to Meiji education are of intrinsic interest, and although their speech cannot be called pure Meiji language, it can be considered representative of the language used by speakers in the Meiji era. In the following, we will use excerpts from recordings of the program to look at two aspects of Meiji language, use of the polite verb *gozaimasu* "be, have," and the pronoun *watakushi* "I."

THE USE OF *"GOZAIMASU"* BY MEIJI WOMEN

First of all, let us consider a transcription of the account of Mano Sakiko who was born in the first year of the Meiji period, 1868 (underlined parts are variants of *gozaimasu*):

(1) *Ma, nagasarebito no yō na wake de <u>gozanshō</u>, haha wa, ma, hon no*

wazuka na kerai to kodomo wo hikitsurete, soshite, nanbu ni shibaraku itan da sō de gozansu yo. Sore kara, nan de gozansu. Atakushi ga Aizu e kaette kimashita no ga yottsu ka itsutsu de gozansu kane. Sore kara, nan de gozansu. Ano, dan dan nan shite kara gakkō ga deki shōgakkō e ittan zansu yo.

Well, maybe I should say that we were wanderers? I was told that my mother, taking a few retainers and the children, resided in the south for a time. Then after that, when I returned to Aizu, I must have been four or five at the time. Then after that, bit by bit, schools were created, starting in the south, and I went to school.

In this segment of speech, *gozansu* (a variant of *gozaimasu*) is used at the end of all the sentences, and *nan de gozaimasu* has been added to the conjunctive *sore kara* (then). Mano uses *gozansu* extensively, since she speaks in an extremely polite manner. Next, let us look at the speech of Fukushima Taki.

(2) *Sono, gakkō tte mo mukashi wa sono, gakkō ja gozaimasen. Mā terakoya de gozaimasu ne....Sensei wa nee, ee, ma, ima de iimasu to kōchō-san de gozaimasu ne. Sore ga o-hitori to, sore kara sono okusan ga mite kudasarun de gozaimasu.*

Even if one calls it a "school," it wasn't one. Well, it was a *terakoya*.[3] . . . The teacher, ah, um, well, what would be the principal today, well there was one and then his wife and they attended to our studies.

In contrast to the speakers above, who make frequent use of *gozansu/gozaimasu*, speakers like Yamada Waka, who end most of their sentences in the plain form, are of special interest.

(3) *Pēji akemasu to ne. Sekai ni go daishū ga aru tte no ne. Sono uchi ni itsutsu ningen no kubi ga itsutsu kaite an da. Kō itsutsu ne, son naka ni nihonjin no kao mo kaite an da yo. Nihonjin wa ajiajin no uchi nari to kaite aru. Sore yoku oboeten da yo ne.*

When I opened the book, it was written that there were five continents. There were (pictures of) five different kinds of people, and there were five explanations. Among these five, there was the face like that of a Japanese. It said that Japanese are among the Asians. That I remember well.

Among the speakers, half of the thirty who appear on the radio program use *gozaimasu*, and the remaining fifteen do not. None of the four men who participated on the program use *gozaimasu*.

The verbal *gozaimasu* is the polite form of *aru* "be/exist," and *de gozaimasu* is the polite form of the copula *de aru/da*. However, there are cases where *de gozaimasu* is used simply to make a sentence more polite:

(4) . . . *no fukusō datta to omoimasu n de gozaimasu.* (Hori Yae)

71

"I thought it was clothing that . . ."
(5) *Katazukimashita n de gozaimasu.* (Nōmi Mutsuko)
"I was married off."
(6) . . . *to iu koto wo shirimashita de gozaimasu.* (Hori Yae)
"I learned that . . ."

The frequent use of *gozaimasu* probably comes from a feeling that . . . *to omoimasu*, "I think . . .," *katazukimashita*, "was married off," and *shirimashita*, "found out" were not polite enough by themselves. Using *gozaimasu* this often comes across as an excessively polite hyperurbanism.

THE USE OF *WATAKUSHI* BY MEIJI WOMEN

Next let us examine the use of first person pronouns. The thirty-four speakers used the following four first person pronouns: *watakushi, atakushi, watashi,* and *atashi.* The frequency of usage is reflected in the table below.

Table 4. Frequency of first-person pronouns		
	Female Speakers	Male Speakers
Watakushi	53	0
Atakushi	55	1
Total	108	1
Watashi	16	7
Atashi	12	2
Total	28	9

Of the first-person pronouns, the more polite *watakushi* and *atakushi,* which we shall call the "*watakushi*-type," are used far more than *watashi* and *atashi,* which we shall call the "*watashi*-type." Men use the *watashi*-type almost exclusively.

Honorifics are also often used when expressing the action or state of a third person.

(7) *Taki Rentarō-san, ano kata ga Doitsu kara o-kaeri ni natte, de, ano , nanka, mōningu nan ka meshite ne.* (Suzuki Nobuko)
When Taki Rentarō returned from Germany, ah, well, he was wearing a morning coat or something.

(8) *Iwamoto-sensei ga kyōdan ni o-tachi ni narimasu to ne. Mo, minna seito wa Kirisuto ga o-tachi ni natta yō datte tottemo sūhai shite ori-*

mashite ne. . . . kō o-yase ni natte rasshaimashite ne. aojiroi o-kao nasutte ne, ika ni mo ne, kōgōshii go-yōsu de, yabure gutsu de ne, kō, o-kamai ni narimasen de. (Matsuoka Shizue)

When Mr. Iwamoto would stand at the podium, well, for the students it was as if Christ were standing there, they worshipped him so much. And then for him to grow so thin, to look so saintly, with torn shoes and not caring for his appearance. . . ."

The speakers above are all talking about their teachers, but honorific expressions are also used when the third party topic of conversation is a friend or a younger student.

(9) *Meiji jogakkō e mairimashite odoroite shimattan desu. Mina-san ga o-deki ni narun de. Ji wa o-jōzu ni o-kaki ni naru shi. . . . iroiro, nani mo, manande rassharun de. . . .* (Fukurai Tatsuko)
When I got to Meiji Girls' School, I was shocked. Everyone was so good at things! They could write well, and they were studying such a variety of things. . . .

(10) *Ryō no tomodachi ga zuibun jitensha o-kai ni narimashite ne.* (Yoshida Toshi)
Many [of my friends in the dormitory] bought bicycles, you know.

Comparing the results of this survey with a 1989 survey conducted on women's language of the Shōwa period ("Josei no hanashi kotoba—terebi no intabyū bangumi kara," 1989, 58), we see that both *watakushi*-type pronouns and *gozaimasu* are used more by women born in Meiji period than women born in the recent Shōwa period. In other words, the language of Meiji women is more polite.

Table 5. Comparison of Meiji and Shōwa women's speech patterns		
	Shōwa	Meiji
Number of Speakers	20	30
Watakushi-type pronouns	74 (38.3%)	108 (79.4%)
Watashi-type pronouns	119 (61.7%)	28 (20.6%)
Use of *gozaimasu*	4 (20%)	15 (50%)
Nonuse of *gozaimasu*	16 (80%)	15 (50%)
Total Phrases	370	445
Number of Usages of *gozaimasu*	6	102
(for *gozaimasu* users)		
Average *gozaimasu*/Phrase	1/61.7	1/4.3

As examples 11 and 12 show, Shōwa women use honorifics very infrequently, and most do not use them at all when talking about friends or younger students.

(11) *O-tomodachi ga kitari suru toki. . . .*
When friends come, or something like that . . .

(12) *Ano, dōkyūsei no shōshaman no tomodachi ga iru n . . .*
Moto ragubī yatte ita . . .
Well, I have a friend who was a classmate and now works at a general trading house. . . . He used to play rugby. . . .

Similarly, when describing the behavior and actions of a third person, Meiji women frequently used honorifics of the *o-VERB ni naru* form, such as *o-kaki ni naru* "write" or *o-utai ni naru* "sing," (26), while Shōwa women used this form only once in the phrase *'o-yasumi ni naru* "rest." On the other hand, there are eight examples of Shōwa women using the honorific suffix *-rare/-rareru*, as in *iwareru* "say" or *kanbyo sareru* "care for," while Meiji women used this form only five times.

To sum up, Meiji women use the more honorific *o-VERB ni naru* form extensively. Shōwa women use honorifics less often than the Meiji women, even though they use the less honorific suffix *-reru/-rareru* comparatively more. By comparing three different aspects of polite language as we have above, we can see that Meiji women use more polite language than women of more recent eras.

Many people criticize recent changes in the way Japanese women speak, saying that the language of women today has become "less polite" or that it has become "coarse." However, if we consider the politeness of the language used by Meiji women as the result of coercive language prescription in the educational system and in society at large, then the changes can be interpreted positively as the result of women feeling freer to express their true selves. When the standard is placed in the context of language as means for women to express themselves freely, then plain, direct speech, with a minimal use of honorifics, is clearly not something to criticize.

NOTES

1. One *sen* is one-hundreth of a *yen*.
2. Yanagida Kunio relates the following about a woman who used words of Chinese origin in the town in Hyogo prefecture where he spent his youth. "There was one woman who used them, and she was a nice person, though I very often heard her criticized for using words of Chinese origin" (*Joshi kyōiku shi*, "A History of Women's Education," NHK).
3. A type of private elementary school of the Edo period usually run by one teacher.

CHAPTER 5
WOMEN'S LANGUAGE IN THE SHŌWA PERIOD: FROM *ASOBASE* TO THE EASING OF GENDER DIFFERENCES

WOMEN'S LANGUAGE BEFORE THE WAR

The early Shōwa period was a time when Japan's increasing militarism coexisted with a kind of decadence fueled by a widespread desire for a temporary escape from anxiety about the possibility of war, and *modan gāru*, "modern girls," and *modan bōi*, "modern boys," strode through the cities, creating new manners and customs. *Modan gāru* instinctively rebelled against things traditionally Japanese, cutting their hair short, wearing Western-style clothing, leading active lives, and exhibiting a strong attraction to Western culture.

Tanaka Sumie writes about the manners and speech of the *modan gāru* (Tanaka 1964, 48–49):

> Among the *moga* and *mobo* (abbreviations of *modan gāru* and *modan bōi*), the women had short hair and wore hats like upturned pots, and the men had long sideburns and wore wide-legged trousers flared like trumpets . . .
>
> One characteristic of *moga* was that they called men *kimi* and themselves *boku*. In line with the new awareness of sexual equality, women being on a par with men, the use of masculine speech forms was their expression of *modān* or "modernity. . . ."
>
> I, too, started to use *kimi*[1] and boku[2] in jest with my school friends after I turned twenty. This was not from any idea of sexual equality . . . but because the masculine style of Mizunoe Takiko, famous for her onstage portrayals of men, was so dashing that I got caught up in it . . . My speech shows how I totally took on a masculine persona:
>
> *Oi, kimi. Hayaku koi yo. Kyō wa bokunchi e tomare yo.*
> "Hey! Come on! Stay at my house tonight!"
>
> *De mo, nee. Okāsan in shikarareru no yo. Onna no ko wa sō yatara ni yoso no ie e tomaru mon ja nai tte.*
> "But, well . . . Mom'll get mad at me. She'll say, 'Girls shouldn't be staying overnight at other people's houses anytime it suits them.'"

> *Kimi no ofukuro wa furui na. Boku ga sukoshi kyōiku shite ageru.*
> "Your mother is really out of date. I'll educate her a little for you."

The following exchange is found in the novel *Shinoyama Shikako no ichi shitai,* which has a *modan gāru* as its main character:

> *Otoko no yō ni ikatsui kata de, habattaku sayū e kaze wo kirinagara guigui mi o yosete kuru nari,*
> Moving freely, strong shouldered like a man, she steadily and rapidly approached,

> *Kimi kā*
> "It's you!"

> *Sōshite wa ha ha to ōzappa na warai wo hanatta*
> Then, she let out a boisterous laugh.

> *Ossoroshiku samui na. Yarikirenee. Oi, taku, ogoranai kaa.*
> "It's awfully cold, ain't it? I just can't stand it! Hey, treat me to a taxi, will you?"

> *Ja, taku ni suru kedo, sono kawari.*
> "All right, I'll treat you but what'll you do for me?"

> *Un. Negiru no wa hito da yo. Ii yo, umaku yatte yara.*
> "Well, I'm the one who should dicker. Never mind. I'll do right by you, O.K?"
> (Muramatsu 1989, 223 [underlining by Endō])

The character described as "strong shouldered like a man" addresses the women to whom she speaks as *kimi* and avoids the use of the first person singular pronoun *watashi* in favor of using *hito* "person." She uses what were held to be exclusively masculine speech forms at the end of her sentences, saying *samui na,* "it's cold, isn't it?" instead of *samui wa nee; yarikirenee,* "can't stand it" instead of *yarikirenai; ogoranai kaa,* "won't you treat me?" instead of *ogoranai;* and *umaku yatte yara*[3]; and she also uses the abbreviation *taku* for *takushi* (taxi).

The stars that played male characters in the Shōchiku Revue became extremely popular with young women who copied their use of masculine language. This was most likely a manifestation of the strong desire of young women for freedom and liberation from male dominance.

However, with the nation preparing for war, hopes of freedom, liberation, and attraction were completely dashed. A woman's duty was to protect hearth and home and send her man off to the "holy war." Her symbol was the *nadeshiko,* the wild Japanese pink, which blooms with grace and beauty, withstanding and enduring all the vagaries of weather. A *Yamato nadeshiko,* a "true daughter of Japan," a beautiful woman embodying all the traditional Japanese feminine virtues, was expected to use a modern version of the same beautiful, refined, graceful speech prescribed in *Onna daigaku.* To turn one's back on using this language was, in fact, to invite criticism and reproach. If we follow the arguments of Yanagi Yae, Dan Michiko, and Morita Tama, social critics who discussed the language used by women in the 1940s, we can see exactly how this behavior was critiqued.

Yanagi Yae thought it was desirable for young women to answer affirmatively with *hai,* stating that the more casual *ee* is an unacceptable response.

(1)   Always answering with *ee,* whether relaxing or on formal occasions, gives an impression similar to always wearing ordinary clothes, no matter the time or place.

(2)   *Ee* is an extremely intimate and familiar answer, and because of that, it sometimes feels too relaxed. (Yanagi 1941, 250)

Yanagi also deplored the use of popular slang. She wrote, "If just one more person were to avoid using those distasteful, vulgar expressions, that would be one less time that they were carelessly brought to one's ears," and "This would be the beginning of progress in practicing good language habits" (Yanagi 1941).

As examples of refined language, Yanagi gave *oshitone* for *zabuton,* "floor cushion," *o-kachin* for *mochi;* "rice cake," and *o-kabe* for tofu, all of which are *nyōbō kotoba* expressions used by elderly women raised during the Meiji period. Under the heading "Receiving Guests," she gave the following helpful advice:

Endeavor not to talk very long and become good at listening. In order not to disturb tranquility of mood or cause discomfort, avoid direct expressions, saying "not good" instead of "bad," and express no more than seven tenths of what is on your mind when giving descriptions and relating feelings. Say everything cheerfully, in a low and flowing voice. When you notice that the conversation has turned to matters of logic, pour fresh tea and offer it. (Yanagi 1941)

The expression *ri ni ochiru,* "turn to matters of logic," reflects the sensibilities of a time when logical thought was considered inappropriate for women.

Morita Tama has the following comments about the speech of young women.

> What I detest the most is a young woman who formally greets someone without blinking an eye. It is preferable for young women to be a little uneven in their speech, and to pause forgetfully and blush a little when uttering the phrases taught by their mothers. Is it because I am old-fashioned that I feel that uttering only four-fifths of what one is thinking and getting the other person to say the rest is more refined than being businesslike and speaking everything that is on one's mind? There is nothing more unpleasant than hearing school girls on trains and buses talking among themselves without reserve or the minimum of decorum. (Morita 1943, 104)

Morita believes that it is pleasing for young women to speak haltingly, to be incomplete in their expression, to lose track of what they were saying, and to act bashful as a result. Even female intellectuals of the Shōwa period encouraged such juvenile behavior in women. This illustrates how persistent and thorough the teachings regarding "faltering" speech for women had been since the Edo period.

After giving examples of newly coined words and popular expressions used by the young people of that time, Dan Michiko enjoined against their use, calling them rough, rude, ugly-sounding, flippant, and shameless. The following sums up her evaluation:

> *Oyoso, imi nai ne/ imi nai wa,* "Well, that's totally meaningless" is a rough expression. Well-mannered gentlemen, married women, and young ladies should take care not to use it.
> *Shitsurei shichau,* "Isn't that rude?" is vulgar. Serious people should not speak it.
> *Shottera/shotteru wa',* "Well, aren't you stuck up?" is not euphonious, so it is irritating.
> *Mochi/mochi-kōsu,* "Of course," is flippant. As it has the ring of *kango,* it is fine for men, but it sounds a little impudent for women.
> *Kare/kanojo,* "he/she": I would like to see people use tasteful Japanese expressions such as a*no kata,* "that esteemed person," *ano hito,* "that person," . . . *san,* "Mr./Mrs./Miss . . .," and . . . *chan* "little Master/Miss. . . ."
> *Chakkari,* "wide-awake, smart," is a disgraceful expression to hear from the mouths of pretty young ladies.
> *Tsukiahanai?* "Keep me company?" / *Chotto kaimono ni maharu no, tsukiahanai?* "I'm going to do a little shopping. Do you want to

keep me company?" And *Iyaiya sau mainichi, tsukiahenai wa* "Well, no. I can't possibly keep you company every day." All these expressions impose association on another person and are unseemly. Their use is unacceptable for young ladies.

(Dan 1943, 40–59)

Dan's criticism of the popular expressions of that time is subjective and emotional as can be seen from her remarks that they are "irritating" and "disgraceful." One wonders how young people reacted to such statements by the intellectuals of the period.

Dan berates women's use of words of Chinese origin and phrases that deviate from the essential "Japaneseness" of the Japanese language. In addition to comments about *mochi* "sure" and *kare/kanojo* "he/she," she adds:

> Considering that women's language should sound as soft as possible, it is better to use *O-tsukaresama*, "Thank you, you must be tired," than *'Gokurōsama*, "Thank you for your hard work." One should try as much as possible to speak in a conversational style rather than in words of Chinese origin. (Dan 1943)

Providing a detailed list of honorific words and titles and giving examples of them, she repeatedly states that women, in particular, should express themselves in a polite manner. In regard to the use of *asobase*, the imperative of a polite form of the verb "to do," she says:

> *Gomen asobase*, "Pardon me"; *o-kaeri asobase*, "Welcome home"; -*o-hajime osobase*, "Please start"; *shōshō gomen asobase*, "Please excuse me a moment"; *o-yari asobase*, "Please do it"; and *o-machi asobase*, "Please wait a moment," etc.—all are pleasing expressions. There is nothing more pleasing than *asobase* when it is used with grace and composure . . . and naturally rolls off the tongue. When it isn't used in that way, it effectively means *asobashi-yagare* (*asobase* with the rough suffix -*yagare*, which sounds rough and impatient). (Dan 1943)

She supports her comments by maintaining that schoolgirls use *asobase* in front of parents and teachers who are strict and fussy about manners. But once away from adults and among themselves, the girls add the extremely vulgar -*yagare* to *asobase* and amuse themselves by purposely using bad language. This was likely a form of rebellion against having politeness and elegance insistently forced upon them, a venting of resentment. Tanaka (1964) also comments along the same lines:

In front of their elders, [schoolgirls] express themselves using *asobase* with complete ease. However, among friends, they amuse themselves by using *gomen asobashagare* "sorry" and *yurushite chabudai* "forgive me"[4] when they speak. (Dan 1943)

At times, Dan even puts forward arguments laced with ironic comparisons with the United States, Japan's military foe at that time. This can be seen in the following argument regarding the use of *-ko*[5] in women's names.

Ko denotes a woman of rank, and since the daughters of commoners do not have rank, it should not be used in their names. Because adding *ko* makes a name sound good, everyone has started using it recently. However, saying *nani nani ko de gozaimasu*, "I am So-and-So-*ko*," means the same thing as *Nani nani sama de gozaimasu*, "I am honorable So-and-So," so it is best to omit *ko* and say *nani nani de gozaimasu*, "I am So-and-So" when in the company of superiors and elders. . . . You may feel that this is bothersome, yet it is due to such practices that the Japanese nation has existed for two thousand years. People of newly founded nations could not emulate this even if they wanted to. (Dan 1943)

Dan thus supports her argument by connecting the origin of words to a sense of superiority towards nations with short histories.

The use of the second person pronoun *kimi* and first person pronoun *boku* in women's language was also discouraged as degenerate and proscribed as representative of "masculinization." Hoshina Kōichi (1872–1955) touches upon the use of these words, writing, "Of late, it would seem that girls are also using personal pronouns used by boys, such as *kimi* and *boku*" (Hoshina 1936, 224). In a similar vein Ishii Shōji writes:

Instruction in the spoken language was quite strict in the past, but language seems to have deteriorated recently. Some parents may lament that the careful language instruction they provide in the home is undone by their children's peers. Meanwhile, educators claim that the attention that they give to the spoken language is undone at home.

Kimi and *boku*, once a troubling aspect of the language of female students, are never used at school these days. Good students say that none of their friends use such words. However, even these students sometimes use them at home after school. In such cases, I can only hope that parents in particular will pay attention. (Ishii 1941, 232)

Although both the schools and the parents place the responsibility for language training on each other, the fact remains that girls are using *kimi* and *boku*. Furthermore, both parents and educators maintain that this usage should not be tolerated.

Kindaichi Kyōsuke (1882–1971) stated that honorifics are the finest aspect of the Japanese language and have a beauty of a kind not seen in the languages of advanced countries in the West. He maintained that "women's language is particularly subtle and delicate," adding, "Recently, it has been noted that Japanese women are superior to the other women of the world in terms of their beauty and quality. The relationship between the correct language of Japanese women and the Japanese feminine ideal is a rare phenomenon in the world" (Kindaichi 1942, 293). Kindaichi ties the forced acceptance of the traditional feminine ideal for war purposes with women's language. However, in real life, there were examples of women's language that deviated from the prescriptions of Kindaichi Kyōsuke and other commentators. Kindaichi did not hide his irritation:

> And yet, what is this trend among educated modern Japanese women to carelessly reject honorifics? Is it that they do not cherish the ways of Japanese women and intend to change to American ways? This is a sad state of affairs. In some homes, children are made to use [the Western-derived words] *mama* and p*apa*, and for this, we can blame women's frivolous lack of awareness, since mothers are responsible for their children's language.... Whatever the case, in order to become a full-fledged Japanese adult woman, one must first learn traditional Japanese women's language, and the exquisite honorifics which are unmatched throughout the world. (Kindaichi 1942, 16)

From this we can see that there was already a noticeable trend among women to drop honorifics.

When a society is thoroughly steeped in the mystique of war, some intellectuals can become remarkably irrational. Dan advocated refinement and gracefulness, yet used vulgar irony to deride Japan's military foes, and although he did not' make any direct comparisons, Kindaichi proclaimed that the ways of Japanese women are superior to all other women and that their language has no equal in the world.

DIMINISHING GENDER DISTINCTIONS

Although intellectuals continuously and repeatedly preached that Japanese women's language was graceful and a model for other women of the world, there was one educator who believed it unnecessary to differentiate between

81

the sexes in elementary school writing instruction. Ashida Enosuke (1873–1951) wrote:

> Just as men and women differ from each other in their physical characteristics, they also differ in their ways of thinking. One is logical, while the other is emotional. It therefore goes without saying that their styles of writing differ. However, in elementary school there is no need to give this undue attention. . . . If girls naturally have their own way of learning, teaching both sexes the same inevitably leads to their doing things differently. It is disgraceful for writing to be purposely weak merely because it is the work of a girl. (Ashida 1973, 450–51)

Although Ashida labels the male sex as logical and the female as emotional and limits his scope to elementary school, his criticism of weak writing most likely indicates a belief that the emphasis on femininity and weakness in girls' education was excessive.

In a similar vein, Ishiguro Yoshimi (1899–1980) discussed the changes in women's language from three aspects:

> Women's use of difficult and inelegant words of Chinese origin has been considered unfeminine throughout history. However, the popularization of women's education since the Meiji period means that girls who have received specialized higher education equal to that of boys now feel free to use Chinese words, with the result that these have become increasingly common in women's speech and writing. This is upsetting the tradition of a gentle and elegant women's language. Moreover, increasing numbers of women, traditionally confined to housework and the rearing of children, have come out of the house and taken up all sorts of occupations since the end if the Meiji period and the early Taishō period. Recently women have even made inroads into fields that would have been unthinkable in the past. It is due to these factors that women's language has changed significantly.
>
> And if I may add something more, recently the war and other factors have led women to favor things that do not restrict activity or movement, particularly clothing such as *monpe* (traditional baggy work pants gathered at the ankles) and trousers in their daily lives, and this has had a notable influence on their speech.
>
> For the many reasons I have given, women's language is gradually becoming sexless and more masculine. In other words, women's language is in danger of being lost.
>
> The simplification and refinement of women's language suits today's lifestyle and as such, it should happen. Yet I hope that we would make the utmost effort to prevent the disappearance of feminine language. (Ishiguro 1943, 232)

This criticism was written near the end of the war, as people's daily lives were being disrupted by the results of Japan's military ventures. It was a time when women were forced to put aside their kimonos and don *monpe* and trousers to participate in fire prevention drills and fight for a place on crowded trains as they traveled to buy the day's rations. Though they may have been called *Yamato nadeshiko*, they could no longer do what they had to do using honorifics such as *asobase* and *zaamasu*. Social demands forced women to become active, and this was reflected in their language. Ishiguro, who was the first to recognize this shift, analyzed it as a neutering or masculinization of women's language. It is likely that Ishiguro was also the first person to sound the alarm regarding the potential loss of women's language.

The end of the war in 1945 brought significant changes to Japan, its society, and its people. Women, who had taken the places of men in factories and scrounged for food to keep their families from starving, confidently made their entry into postwar society. Due to the collapse of the family system, the traditional role of serving men was becoming a thing of the past as people gradually came to understand the equal rights of men and women guaranteed under the new constitution.

This, of course, led to changes in women's language. Furuya Tsunatake is taken aback at the use by "young women intellectuals" of words incorporating many unfamiliar-sounding Chinese characters:

> They talk about their thoughts and feelings with expressions such as *hōhai to shite okottan desu*, "which surged forth," *totemo gekietsu na kuchō de*, "in a very vehement tone," and *sono kangaekata o hasai sureba*, "reducing that concept to its constituent parts." However, it isn't certain that these young women have full command of these expressions. It is likely only that they forgot traditional women's language in the midst of war.
> (Furuya 1946, 34 [underlining by Furuya])

In taking exception to women's use of words of Chinese origin, he is expressing feelings that are reactionary compared to those of Ishiguro, who during the war saw this usage in a somewhat positive light as the result of the spread of education.

In 1948, the third year after the war, the journalist Suzuki Bunshirō caused controversy when he proposed the "abolition of women's language" during a radio broadcast. To paraphrase Suzuki, he was of the opinion that women's language is the idiom born of the views expressed in Kaibara Ekiken's *Onna daigaku*, which maintained that, due to their sex, women were to obey, to be gentle and charming in all things, and to use the *teyodawa kotoba* that arose out of the geisha quarters of the Meiji period. Furthermore,

Suzuki explains that women in Japan, just because they were women, were expected to use *asobase kotoba*, as well as attaching the honorific prefix *o-* to such words as *denwa*, "telephone," *kōcha*, "black tea," and *kōhī*, "coffee," such as *o-denwa*, (honorific *o* + telephone), *o-kōcha* (*o* + black tea), and o-*kōhī* (*o* + coffee).

> However, in this time of individual equality and the equal rights of men and women, the existence of such decidedly different language styles for the sexes is equivalent to women breaking down these rights with their speech. While language is the expression of thought, it has at the same time the power to give shape to thoughts. . . . The learned Kaibara's soul is now at rest, and it is absurd to expect women to use language as flimsy as a geisha's ornate underskirt. When we look at it this way, it is not at all strange that women started wearing men's trousers during the war, and, if we can accept that, then it is fine for them to wear the "men's trousers" of language, too. (Suzuki 1948, 60–61)

Suzuki urges women to abandon feminine language and suggests using the form . . . *de arimasu* (the formal form of the copula) as a replacement for polite forms such as *de gozaimasu*. In a roundtable discussion, "A New Femininity," published in the July 1948 volume of the magazine *Fujin kōron* (Women's Public Opinions), Hirabayashi Taiko gives the following rebuttal:

> I wonder whether the expressions suggested by Mr. Suzuki, *sō de arimasu*, "it is so," and *sō de arimashita*, "it was so," are, as he seems to think, suitable as part of woman's language or that it is even possible they might be. . . . Should not these expressions, rather, be construed as neutral? In other words, I think that this is a kind of unification in which masculine language dispossesses feminine language. . . .Would it not be better to go on creating more feminine expressions instead, and for woman to use feminine language and men masculine?

Hirabayashi trivializes Suzuki's proposal to abolish feminine language with its vestiges of feudalism and to democratize language by characterizing it as an attempt to pit men's language against women's language.

Suzuki's proposal was well ahead of its time, since traces of feminine speech styles remain in the Japanese language even now, more than fifty years after his controversial radio broadcast.

Spurred by the establishment of legal equality, some women threw off many prewar social constraints. Hirabayasahi claimed that these women rejected "femininity," as well as "smok[ing] cigarettes, drink[ing] beer, us[ing] *boku* and *kimi*, and not feeling the least bit nervous around men" (Tanaka 1956, 78). The language of women was certainly changing, even though it was not the self-conscious language reform Suzuki promoted. Male intellectuals praised this change with comments such as, "Female students have became outspoken" (Yoshida 1955, 167). "Having just been liberated, they are brimming with energy," and "At a certain meeting, I saw a woman around the age of twenty speaking unapologetically in front of a large number of men, and I was struck with admiration" (Ōkubo 1956a, 37). With their words of praise, these men commended the speech of young women who used language in ways that had been proscribed by Morita Tama only ten years before.

It was not only the language of women that had changed. Not hiding his surprise at the feminization of men's language, Mashimo Saburō (1948) writes:

> It is a curious phenomenon that boys are increasingly using the sentence-final emotive particles generally employed by women.
> I am often surprised that the speech of educated people living in Tokyo is moving closer to feminine language, and radio talk shows are particularly bad in this respect. One often hears the following expressions:

no	*sō deshita no*	"that's right"
yo	*sō desu yo*	"that's right!"
no ne	*sō datta no ne*	"that's right, isn't it"
		(Mashimo 1948, 80)

The March 1953 volume of *Fujin kōron* contains an article that proposed abolishing gender distinctions in language. The author maintained, "It is best to get rid of any distinctions between men's and women's language. There is nothing odd about either men or women using the polite verbal endings -*masu* (positive nonpast form), -*masen* (negative nonpast form), *desu* (the copula) and *de wa arimasen* (negative of the copula)" (145). Furthermore, Nagano Masaru states, "As men and women achieve real equal rights in society, the characteristics of women's language based on differences in social status and education level—that is, the social conditions—will gradually disappear" (Nagano 1955, 81).

Yazaki Genkurō also comments on the convergence of women's and men's language in his work on the future of the Japanese language.

> Recently, women have been making rapid progress socially. . . .
> As they do so, the gap between women's and men's language is shrinking. However, women's language seems to be moving to-

wards men's language. To put it another way, women's language is becoming somewhat rougher ... while, on the other hand, men's language is becoming softer. .... Although it is not clear if women's language is coming to resemble men's, or men's language is coming to resemble women's, whichever the case may be, the gap between them is gradually shrinking. In any event, this is a trend that we should applaud. Since these are times of sexual equality, it is not commendable to have an excessively wide gap between the linguistic usage of the two sexes. (Yazaki 1960, 209)

This "rapprochement," the crossover of styles, in which women's and men's language come to resemble each other, started soon after the war and continued through the 1950s and 1960s.

PUBLIC ATTITUDES TOWARD WOMEN'S LANGUAGE

Ever since the end of World War II, newspapers and broadcasting stations have often carried out public opinion surveys on language. In 1980, Japan's government-sponsored broadcasting system, NHK, polled 3,600 people age 16 or older on the question, "What are your feelings about language usage today?" Seventy-five percent of the people questioned responded, and multiple answers were allowed. The results showed the following percentages of respondents agreeing with the statements they were given (NHK 1980, 1).

(1) The language of women has become rougher. - 68%
(2) Peculiar ways of talking and strange popular expressions are becoming more common. - 60%
(3) There are more foreign language-based words and foreign loanwords with obscure meanings. - 51%
(4) Correct use of honorifics is becoming increasingly rare. - 50%

These results could be a manifestation of the "reactionary climate" against postwar language changes that Miyaji Yutaka (1924–) commented on as early as 1957. He stated:

Since the war, well-defined vertical class relationships have been replaced with relatively familiar relationships. Furthermore, it is becoming increasingly difficult to isolate women's language at a time when the husband and wife are no longer in a master-servant relationship but interact as friends. .... In spite of this, women master the various ways of adapting their language, mostly with respect to honorific expressions, as they grow into adulthood. I do not believe that this is desirable state of affairs for a modern society. (Miyaji 1957, 25)

Miyaji thus sees the requirement for women to master numerous forms of honorifics as counterproductive.

In a 1986 survey, NHK asked 2,159 people age 16 or older questions similar to the ones asked in 1980. The top replies among the 1,549 people who responded to the survey were (NHK 1986, 2):

(1) Peculiar ways of talking and strange popular expressions are becoming more common. - 55%

(2) The language of women has become rougher. - 53%

(3) There are more foreign-language based words and foreign loanwords with obscure meanings. - 45%

(4) Correct use of honorifics is becoming increasingly rare. - 43%

(5) The use of incorrect language is increasing. - 34%

It is interesting to note that agreement with the statement, "The language of women has become rougher," had decreased by 15 percent. Looking at the figures more closely, we can see that this means the number of people who agree with the statement has decreased by 20 percent in six years. One possibility is that society has become accustomed to the changes in the speech of women. Another is that women's language is not as coarse as it was in 1980. However, language change is a historical fact and cannot be reversed quickly. Thus, we can safely interpret the results as meaning that society has become accustomed to and accepting of changes in women's language.

A number of surveys have been done on both the differentiation and convergence of men's and women's language. In 1955, the publishing house Ōtsuki Shoten placed a questionnaire about trends in language usage in the first edition of *Kōza Nihongo* (Symposium on Japanese). With return postage paid, 2,455 people answered the survey. Among the questions was: "What is your view on the differentiation of men's and women's language?" Results compiled from the possible responses are noted below (*Kōza Nihongo* 1955, 232).

(1) There should be more differentiation. - 11%

(2) The status quo is acceptable. - 56%

(3) There should be no differentiation. - 31%

(4) No answer. - 2%

Thirty-one percent of respondents replied that there should be no differentiation between men's and women's language. In other words, a third of responses agreed with Suzuki Bunshirō's proposal to abolish women's language. However, the majority of respondents did not agree and favored a continued distinction between men's and woman's language.

In 1983, more than thirty years after the war, NHK conducted a survey to find out how attitudes towards woman's language differed by generation (NHK 1984, 16). The survey was completed by 1,000 prefectural and municipal government employees from around the country who were attending the National Advertisement and Publicity Research Conference. In this survey, 84 percent of respondents replied that differences between men's and women's language were disappearing. When asked what they thought of this change, over 50 percent replied that it was undesirable.

In 1986, NHK questioned the households of 363 women employed outside the home in the Tokyo metropolitan area, in the "Survey on Working Women's Attitudes Towards Language" (NHK 1986, 18). Note that 76 percent of respondents agreed with the survey question, "What do you think of the statement: 'Women's language is being masculinized'?"

Agree	30%
Somewhat agree	46%
Somewhat disagree	6%
Disagree	6%
Neither	13%

Building upon this question, the survey offered specific examples of sentence endings thought to be exclusively used by women and asked, "Some people say that recently these phrases of women's language . . . *shita wa*, . . . *da wa*, . . . *ne*, . . . *na no*, and . . . *koto*, are being dropped. What do you think about this statement?" The responses are:

Agree	23%
Somewhat agree	41%
Somewhat disagree	11%
Disagree	15%
Neither	9%

In short, 76 percent of working women thought at the time that women's language was becoming more "masculine," and 64 percent thought that the use of sentence final particles was decreasing.

Again, the survey asked, "Should we retain the expressions that are used exclusively by woman at the end of sentences or not?" The responses indicate that the total number of women who believe expressions exclusive to women should be retained (1 and 2 combined) is higher than those who do not (3, 4, and 5 combined).

(1) Should be retained	16%
(2) Rather be retained than not	30%
(3) Rather not be retained	11%
(4) No need to retain	26%
(5) Undecided	17%

Next, let us take a look at the results of a survey of 3,000 people over the age of 16, 1,500 men and 1,500 women, carried out in 1995 by the Agency for Cultural Affairs under the title "Public Opinion Poll Regarding the Japanese Language." There were 2,212 valid responses.

Here are the answers elicited by asking the respondents to indicate which statement most closely matches their opinion regarding the decreasing distinctions between the language usage of men and women.

(1) There should be no differences	9.8%
(2) Change is natural and inevitable	41.2%
(3) There should be differences	44.1%
(4) Not sure	4.0%
(5) Do not know	0.9%

The number of respondents who favor the disappearance of gender distinctions (1) combined with the number who passively consent to their disappearance (2) is greater than the number who favor retention of gender distinctions (3). This is the first time we have seen the respondents who actively or passively favor the elimination of gender distinctions outnumbering those who favor their retention.

Table 6. Differences in language usage by men and women (by sex)			
	Total	Males	Females
Responses	2,212	1,016	1,196
No difference preferred	9.8%	9.3%	10.2%
Change natural	41.2%	41.4%	41.0%
Differences preferred	44.1%	45.4%	43.1%
Cannot say	4.0%	3.1%	4.7%
Do not know	0.9%	0.8%	1.0%

Source: Agency for Cultural Affairs 1995, 16.

Table 7. Differences in language usage by men and women (by sex and age)

Age	Males						Females					
	16-19	20-29	30-39	40-49	50-59	60+	16-19	20-29	30-39	40-49	50-59	60+
Responses	68	129	150	217	195	257	63	148	232	275	215	263
No differences preferred	10.3%	12.4%	6.0%	7.4%	8.2%	11.7%	15.9%	13.5%	7.8%	10.2%	8.8%	10.3%
Change Natural	63.2%	52.7%	40.0%	44.7%	35.9%	32.3%	57.1%	52.7%	39.2%	39.3%	41.4%	33.5%
Differences preferred	25.0%	31.8%	46.7%	45.6%	51.3%	52.1%	19.0%	29.1%	47.0%	45.1%	46.0%	48.7%
Cannot say	1.5%	3.1%	6.7%	1.8%	4.1%	1.9%	6.3%	4.7%	5.6%	4.4%	3.3%	4.9%
Do not know			0.7%	0.5%	0.5%	1.9%	1.6%		0.4%	1.1%	0.5%	2.7%

Source: Agency for Cultural Affairs 1995, 17.

Although we cannot see a distinct divergence between men and women overall, when we break down the categories by age, we find that those in their twenties and thirties support or accept the disappearance of exclusively feminine language in overwhelmingly greater numbers than other age groups: 73.5 percent of teen-aged males and 73.0 percent of teen-aged females hold these views. Despite the nearly equal percentages of support, more young men support the changes passively, while young women express more active support. In other words, young women in their teens are the group that most eagerly desires and supports the trend towards diminishing gender differences in language. Only 19.0 percent think that there should be difference, a particularly low number compared to other age groups. These results can be understood as self-justification by young women who have been criticized and censured for using rough and masculine language.

This question follows a series of seven statements, such as "language has deteriorated," to which respondents are asked to reply either affirmatively or negatively. The top three statements that received affirmative responses are related to language change (Agency for Cultural Affairs 1995, 5):

	Agree	Disagree
(1) We need to be aware of the influence that the language used on television and radio has on children.	8.4%	7.6%
(2) Language today has deteriorated.	73.6%	19.6%
(3) The state needs to make efforts to preserve the correctness and beauty of the Japanese language.	71.5%	19.8%

These and the other seven questions that require either affirmative or negative answers can be considered leading questions. Presenting the questions in this way increases the number of people who answer "agree," even if they are not usually concerned with the issue. The NHK surveys employ a similar method of questioning in which respondents are asked to select from opinions already presented. Although this is a questionable way of ascertaining opinions, the manner of presentation reflects the mood of the times. However, it is important to note that the nature of the opinions offered by each survey is significantly different: the seven questions do not refer to women's language directly. The researchers seem to have developed an awareness of the discriminatory nature of singling out women's language and of the way in which leading questions can plant false ideas in people's minds, such as the preconceived notion that women's language is coarse.

LANGUAGE IN THE WORKPLACE

Many women are undoubtedly suspicious of and displeased with the differences between the language they use in their daily lives and the linguistic forms and expressions that the dictionaries and grammar books have hitherto prescribed exclusively for women. For example, the fourth edition of the *Sanseido Kokugo Dictionary* (Sanseido National Language Dictionary, 1992) contains the following entries, with [W] indicating items said to be "women's language."

> *O-jiya*: (noun) [W] a porridge of rice and vegetables.
> . . . *ka shira*: (sentence-final particle) [W] a construction that expresses a questioning mood: *iku ka shira* "I wonder if we will go," or *kore wa dō ka shira* "How would this be?"

Yet *o-jiya* is used by men and women alike. Furthermore, this research shows that . . . *ka shira* is currently often used by men.

Likewise, in his work *Hataraku josei no kotoba* Japanese language scholar Horii Reiichi lists words used in the apparel industry, where women have traditionally predominated, as women's language terms (Horii 1992). He also characterizes secretarial work and banking as typical female occupations and presents terms used in those service jobs as women's language. Why are such terms labeled "the language of working women"? Why are terms relating to Japanese clothing, such as *o-kumi*, "gusset," and *miyatsukuchi*, "the open section under the arm of a kimono," considered to be women's language? These seem to be convenient manipulations of the truth. In fact, my own research grew out of questions about the differences between actual usage and the so-called "women's language" prescribed by men.

How do women in contemporary Japan use language? In order to avoid confusing the issue with dialects and generational differences, we will look at the language used by women in the greater Tokyo metropolitan area in their daily lives.

The research discussed below was carried out by a total of nine researchers, members of the Modern Japanese Research Association and a researcher from the National Academy of Language Research. We began our study by taping naturally occurring discourse in the workplace. We asked each of three or four informants from various age brackets between twenty and fifty to record three hours of spoken language: a preliminary meeting, a project meeting, an employees' meeting, a telephone conversation, and casual talk with coworkers during a break. Researchers then transcribed the audiotapes and produced a digital database from which to analyze the state of women's speech in the workplace.[6] In the following, I will summarize our findings on the use of response terms that reply to questions and requests for confirmation by the speaker.

The possible affirmative responses in Japanese, in descending order of formality, are *haa*, *hai*, *ee*, and *un*. According to the grammar books and dictionaries, women should use the more polite forms, while men should use the less polite. Yet our recorded conversations tell a different story. Males and females all use all the forms, and which form they use depends on the relationship between the speakers, their relative ages, their relative social ranks, and the overall formality of the situation.

For example, a female student answers a female professor's comment with *hai*, and a female editor answers a male writer's opening statement in the same way. Yet *ee* is used in a preliminary meeting between two workplace colleagues, and a member of an editorial staff having lunch with a university professor responds to his question with *un*.

A female high school teacher in her thirties, recorded in interactions with male colleagues ranging in age from their thirties to their sixties, uses all three forms in patterns similar to those of the men she is speaking to. Her use of the negative responses *iie* and *iya*, "no," is also similar to that of her male colleagues.

Similarly, a female university professor in her fifties uses the same affirmative replies as her male colleague in his sixties, and in roughly the same proportions.

When a female magazine editor speaks with the male owner of the publishing company, both use *un* more than any other response. Yet the publisher uses *hai* a greater percentage of the time than his employee does.

However, in different situations with different addressees, the editor's use of *un* decreases. When she conducts a formal negotiation with the operations department manager of an outside company, she says *un* only once, and otherwise uses *hai* and *ee*. In this case, the older male informant uses *hai* most frequently, while the younger female informant uses the less polite *ee* most frequently. In this situation, the young editor holds the power to place an order, while the supplier, who is older but who wants the order to be placed, is the weaker party. Here we see not a woman speaking more politely to a man because of her sex, but a man speaking more politely to a woman because she has the upper hand in this conversation.

In conclusion, we can analyze the affirmative replies of women in the workplace as follows: First, *un* occurs most often. Second, there are no gender differences in the replies. Third, the replies reflect the power relationships between the speakers.

Next, let us look principally at sentence-final forms in discourse, using the speech of an editor in her forties. When speaking with one of the writers, a university professor in his sixties, she uses very polite forms, not only *hai* but also *gozaimasu*, while the professor uses rather plain language.

> F: *Ja, dō iu junjo de hajimemashō ka.*
> "Well, in what order shall we start?"
> M: *Moshi yatte kureru nara, boku no-, are de mo yatte moraō ka na.*
> "If you'd like to do me a favor, I'd like my . . . I'd like to have you do that one."
> F: *Hai. Kore, 151 to 310 wa ichiji-kō de.*
> "Yes. This is no. 151 and this is no. 10. They are originals."
> M: *Hai.*
> "I see."
> F: *Eeto, sorekara 250 mo kyo hajimete de gozaimasu yone.*
> "And, uh, after that, also no. 250 is a new one today, isn't it."

However, in a lunchtime chat with other members of the editorial staff, the editor speaks in a more casual tone. When speaking with her colleagues in an informal setting, she uses the sentence-final particles *na(a)*, "isn't it?," and . . . *ka na(a)*, "I wonder if . . .," even though the *Nihon bunpō daijiten* (Japan's Great Grammar Dictionary, 1971) describes sentence final particles *ka na{a}* and *na{a}* as expressions used exclusively by men. When we compare the speech styles that she uses in conferring with the older male author and with her own colleagues, she seems to be two different people.

From the editor's speech, it is clear her speech is polite in the editorial meeting not because she is a woman, but because she is speaking with lower status as an editor conversing with a writer. In the casual conversation among coworkers, the youngest woman uses the formula copula *desu* twice, undoubtedly because she is interacting with older colleagues, but that is about as formal as the conversation gets.

When we also look at conversations between a government employee in her forties and her male section manager, we find that she speaks formally to her supervisor when they are discussing an upcoming meeting, while he gives only informal replies, but that both speakers use informal speech patterns when the conversation switches to a discussion of what to serve at the meeting. Interestingly, the male speaker uses a sentence-final *no*, the supposedly "feminine" informal form of the . . . *no da* explanatory predicate, and the supposedly feminine phrase *ii ja nai* "wouldn't it be all right?"

When we observe language as it is actually spoken in the workplace, we find women using language that is neither more polite nor more honorific than that of men. Of course, our discussion has been limited to language in the workplace and does not cover language in the home or in the larger society, so it is impossible to make blanket generalizations about women's speech on the basis of this evidence. In order to obtain a true picture of the current state of women's language, we will need to observe more kinds of people in more situations.

In any case, so-called "women's language" was originally described and prescribed by men on the basis of the speech of small subgroups of women and historical documents. Perhaps instead of merely accepting the descriptions and prescriptions of men, women will now define themselves by recording the language of today as they know it and point out the aspects that have been ignored by male scholars.

CONTEMPORARY TRENDS

Commentators writing about the Japanese language often cite conversations in novels to illustrate differences between men's and women's language. Kindaichi Haruhiko states that it is possible to figure out which speaker in the following conversation is male and which is female, simply from the sentence patterns and vocabulary:

> (1) *Anata, anata nara dō suru?*
> "Dear, what would you do if it happened to you?"
> (2) *Dō suru tte nani ga da ne?*
> "What do you mean, what would I do?"
> (3) *Moshimo, anata no bōya ga korosareta to shitara, yappari sekentei wo massaki ni kangaeru?*
> "If your son were killed, would you first wonder what the neighbors would think?"
> (4) *Baka na koto wo iu mon ja nai yo.*
> "This isn't something you should make stupid remarks about."
> (5) *Sonna shinpai shita koto nai no?"*
> "Haven't you ever had those kinds of worries?"
> (Kindaichi 1988, 36)

In the preceding conversation, the language used in the odd-numbered sentences makes it clear that the speaker is female, while the speaker in the even-numbered sentences is just as obviously male.

However, recently one finds more and more conversations in which it is impossible to tell the sex of the speaker from the spoken dialogue along, as in this excerpt from Yoshimoto Banana's *Kicchin* (Kitchen).

(1) *Ame ga furu ka na watashi ga iu to*
"I said, 'Wonder if it will rain,' and . . ."
(2) *Iya, harete kurun ja nai? to Sōichirō wa itta*
"Sōichirō said, 'No, it should begin to clear up, don't you think?'"

(Yoshimoto 1988, 39)

The dialogue here would not sound unnatural, even if the tag lines were reversed.

Next, here is a conversation that appears in the 1995 Akutagawa Prize-winning work, *Kono hito no iki* (Her Territory) by Hosaka Kazushi.

(1) *Biiru mō chotto nomō ka*
"Why don't we drink a bit more beer?"
(2) *Ii kedo*
"Well, O.K, but . . ."
(3) *Jikan, daijōbu?*
"Do you have time?"
(4) *Sore wa heiki.*
"No problem."
(5) *Danna-san te itsumo nanji gurai ni kaette kuru no?*
"About what time does your husband usually come home?"
(6) *Osoi yo*
"Late!"

(Hosaka 1995)

Lines (1), (3), and (6) are spoken by a woman, and (2), (4), and (5) by a man. Except for the reference to "your husband," we would not be able identify the speaker's gender from her speech.

On September 12, 1995, the financial newspaper *Nihon Keizai Shinbun* reported that the language of women in the subtitles of movies had changed:

> Where traditionally *Atakushi de wa muri da to ossharu no*, "Are you saying that it is impossible for me?" is now *Watashi ja muri da to*. *Dōshite na no kashira*, "I wonder what it could it be?" has become *Naze*, "Why?" and *Kakatte irasshai yo*, "Why don't you attack me!" has become *Kakatte koi*.

In the western *The Quick and the Dead*, actress Sharon Stone strikes a villain in the face and utters an expletive. The subtitle that accompanies the words is *manuke*, "fool."[7]

Ore, a first person pronoun that was considered to be for the exclusive use of men and unsuitable for women, has even been incorporated into *waka*, a Japanese poetic form.

Sakadachi shite omae ga ore o nagameteta
   tatta ichido kiri no ano natsu no koto.
"Standing opposite, you gazed at me
   A one-time—only happening of that summer past."
                                                    (Kōno 1991)

This usage is reminiscent of a junior high school girl saying *Omotee naa, ore no kaban,* "It's heavy—my school bag!" as reported in the *Yomiuri Shinbun* (1995), a nationally circulated newspaper. Along with uses of "masculine" pronouns and verbal endings, an increasing number of women use the plain imperative, formerly considered to be for exclusively male use and unbecoming for women, and the sentence-final particles *zo* and *ze.* I recall an NHK television announcer yelling the imperative *Tsukkomeee!* "Charge!" and the catch phrase *Dōjō suru nara, kane wo kure!* "Give me money rather than sympathy!" The saying was used by young girls and was selected as 1994's Most Popular Expression (Endō 1995d, 46). Similar examples are easy to find. Below are two examples from the Mainichi newspaper.

Yo no naka ni wa otokotachi no shiranai nettowāku ga arun da ze.
"There are networks in this world that men don't know about."
(March 12, 1994)

Kō natta to shiranakatta zo.
"I didn't realize that it had worked out like this." (April 23, 1996)

Many passengers in cars driven by women have undoubtedly heard their drivers utter all sorts of "language exclusive to men." On the other hand, we find more and more examples of men using "feminine" language. Some examples are listed below.

(1) *Eraku hanashi ga chigau no yo ne.* (Uno 1971, 90)
"That wasn't our understanding, you know."
(2) *Watashi no koto eiga ni tsurete ikimasu no.* (Uno 1971, 90).
"Someone's taking me to a movie."
(3) *Rie-san wo butai ni dō kashira.* (Bandō 1994b)
"How about Rie for a part (in theatre)."
(4) *De mo, geijutsuteki insupirēshion wa kotoba no kabe o koeru wa ne, yappari.* (Bandō 1994a)
"But creative inspiration is understood even when words aren't, don't you think, really?"
(5) *Tatoe ōsama de arō ga, shushō de arō ga mappira gomen na no ne.* (Bandō 1994a)
"It doesn't matter if it's the king or the prime minister, you can count me out!"

(6) *Sono hon totte.* (Inoue 1994)
"Fetch that book!"
(7) *Dare ga kaita no.* (Bandō 1994a)
"Who wrote this?"
(8) *Ii tenki ne.* ("Kotoba no seisa sarani chiisaku," [Bandō 1994a])
"Nice weather, isn't it?" (Underlined by Endō)

The younger generation is likely unaware that (6), (7), and (8) were originally forms exclusive to women. To make a command, men would have said
totte kure, while women were supposed to say *totte kudasai, totte chōdai*, or to
omit the auxiliary verb and simply say *totte.* In the case of (7), the sentence-
final particle *no* was also relegated as exclusive to women, and men were
expected to use phrases such as: *dare ga kaita* or *dare ga kaita no ka.* The direct
attachment in (8) of the final-particle *ne* to a noun was also labeled as usage
exclusive to women, and men were expected to say *ii tenki da ne.*

Usage is changing so quickly that additional explanation is necessary. Kindaichi Haruhiko has dubbed this phenomenon a mutual extension,
or "asexualization," of women using men's language, and men using wom-
en's language (Kindaichi 1998). However, one could interpret these changes
as a return to ancient times where there were no gender differences in the
Japanese language.

NOTES

1. *Kimi* is a second person pronoun traditionally considered suitable for
male speakers to use to address persons of the same or lower social rank.

2. *Boku* is a first person pronoun traditionally considered suitable for male
speakers to use in casual exchanges with those of the same or lower social rank.

3. *Yara* is an enumerative particle, considered masculine, current at this
time.

4. Incidentally, the practice of using *chabudai* "low dining table" in place of
chōdai "please do" in the phrase *yurushite chabudai* is analogous to the use of expressions such as *gambaringo* ("I'll do my best" where verb final *ru* is replaced by *ringo*
= "apple" and *konban wain* "Good evening," where the final *wa* is replaced by *wain*
= wine) in *Obotchama kotoba* and *Chama go*, short-lived forms of slang that gained
popularity among children in 1988 and 1989.

5. An affix used in women's names; literally meaning "child." It no longer
has the honorific connotation that Dan ascribes to it, and for a long time, especially in
the middle decades of the 20th century, it was an integral part of most female names.
However, it has become less common in recent years.

6. For further details see Gendai Nihongo Kenkyūkai, *Josei no kotoba shokuba
hen* (Hitsuji, 1997).

7. *Manuke*, a "blockhead" or "fool" is a semivulgar expression unlikely to be
favored as an example of demure women's language.

CHAPTER 6
WOMEN'S LANGUAGE TODAY:
WOMEN COINING WORDS, WOMEN PLAYING
WITH LANGUAGE

As the feminist movement spread throughout the world in the 1970s, Japanese women, whose verbal expression had been largely suppressed throughout history, become increasingly independent and therefore empowered to speak out. Women who had been subjected to derogatory male-invented epithets discovered their own power to create disparaging or jocular terms for men and other playful forms of language. This newfound freedom was exercised not only by young women, but also by women old enough to have undergone training in "proper, feminine" speech.

WOMEN AND *RYŪKŌGO*

Before discussing contemporary women's language, let us clearly define the terms we will be using in our analysis, beginning with *ryūkōgo* "catch words," *wakamono-kotoba* "young people's language," and *shingo* "neologisms."

Ryūkōgo are words or phrases popular during a particular period of time. Two early examples from the period preceding World War II are *mobo* and *moga* from the English "modern boy" and "modern girl." During World War II, *hoshigarimasen katsu made wa*, "We will have no selfish desires until the war is won," was a popular saying. In the immediate postwar period, one often heard *binbōnin wa mugi wo kue*, "The poor should eat wheat [instead of rice]." Examples of present-day *ryūkōgo* include *chapatsu* "hair bleached or dyed brown," and *meccha-kawaii*, "awfully cute."

Wakamono-kotoba is sometimes called *wakamonogo* and overlaps with student slang (*kyanpasu-kotoba*, "campus language" or *gakuseigo*, "university student language"), the colloquialisms used by young female office workers ("office ladies" or "OL"), and parts of *kogyarugo* (the speech forms used by *kogyaru* or fashion-obsessed teenage girls). When such slang expressions gain common currency, they enter the domain of *ryūkōgo*.

Shingo or neologisms include two kinds of words: newly coined words or abbreviations, such as *risutora* (from the English "restructuring" and usually referring to the firing of employees) and words or phrases that have been given a new meaning or usage such as *gasu nuki*, which originally

99

meant "deflated" but has come to mean "drained of energy" or "having lost momentum." Many neologisms fall into the categories of *ryūkōgo* or *waka-mono-kotoba*, but not all of them end up as *ryūkōgo*.

These new lexical items are often closely interrelated. The same word may be considered young people's slang from one perspective and ne-ologisms or colloquial expressions from another. Our main focus, therefore, will be *ryūkōgo*. At times we will also take up *wakamono-kotoba*, especially when it overlaps with *ryūkōgo*.

Ryūkōgo was formally known as *hayari-kotoba*, "fashionable lan-guage," and not recommended for use by women. *Onna chōhoki* (1692), one of the manuals of behavior for women that I mentioned in chapters 3 and 4, states that "good housekeepers should not use *hayari-kotoba*, such as *shikato*, 'certainly, for sure,' *gebiru*, 'to coarsen, become vulgar,' and *yaku*, 'be jeal-ous.'" *Shinsen onna yamato daigaku* severely admonishes women that they "should on no account use *hayari-kotoba* or vulgar expressions" (*Onna chōho-ki hoka* 1981, 23).

As late as the middle of the Shōwa era, Yanagi Yae and Dan Michiko advocated the prohibition of *hayari-kotoba*. Yanagi indirectly attempted to discourage women from using *hayari-kotoba*, saying, "If even only one more woman stopped using this undesirable *hayari-kotoba*, if the number of such utterances were reduced even by one, then we would have taken a step to-ward making good usage a reality" (Yanagi 1941, 250). Dan Michiko also repeatedly cites examples of contemporary *ryūkōgo* that should not be used. According to Dan, *mochi*, an abbreviation of *mochiron*, "of course," and *mo-chi-kōsu* (*mochi* with the addition of "course" from "of course,") were "words used by loose women," and it was "a disgrace for young ladies to let *chak-kari*, 'cheeky expressions, impertinent language' pass their lips" (Dan 1943, 40–59).

Men in those days created words to refer to a woman as a member of a married couple. Terms such as *wakazuma*, "young wife," *niizuma*, "new wife," and *ryōsai*, "good wife," are attested, but we have no written records of equivalent terms coined from the female point of view, such as equivalents to "young husband," "new husband," or "good husband." There were also many names for women in the sex trade, such as *baishōfu*, "a woman who sells her sex," *baishunfu*, "a woman who sells her spring (sex)," *shūgyōfu*, "a woman of the ugly trade," *shōfu*, "a woman for play," *meshimori onna*, "a woman who serves rice" (maids at inns who doubled as prostitutes), or *tsuji gimi*, "lady of the crossroads." From this, it is evident that although women were objects named and prescribed by the gender with power, women did not have the autonomy to create names for men. There are a few exceptions, such as *iro* and *mabu*, which the prostitutes of the Edo-era used to refer to their customers, much as modern North American prostitutes refer to their customers as "johns." The prostitute's argot, however, was restricted to the defined world of the pleasure quarters.

Men coined a number of derogatory words for women after the end of the WWII such as *urenokori*, "unsold goods," or *ōrudo-misu*, "old miss," for older unmarried women. It was not until the early 1980s, when Higuchi Keiko coined *sodaigomi*, "large trash," and *nureochiba*, "a wet, fallen leaf," to refer to retired husbands hanging around the house, that words created by women, offensive or otherwise, were brought to public attention (*Gendai yōgo no kiso chishiki* 1986, 1100). Derogatory phrases coined by women to refer to men were covered by the mass media after the International Women's Year in 1975, when the abolition of sexual discrimination became a focus of public debate. Even older women began to realize that, in many ways, they were better off than their husbands, who had lost their power and position in society upon retiring from work.

As described in chapter 3, the *nyōbō-kotoba* of medieval times was an argot developed by women. Although it has been the object of some curiosity throughout history and is praised for its creativity, the only terms from *nyōbō-kotoba* that we know today are names for food, clothing, and kitchenware. If the *nyōbō* created in-group nicknames for the socially more powerful nobles and samurai warriors with whom they had daily contact, no written records of these nicknames remain. Therefore, one of the first widely reported names created by women for men was *sodaigomi*. Since then, young women in particular have created many expressions reflecting the roles, uses, and statuses that they assign to men, such as *Paseri-kun* "Mr. Parsley" (the garnish that is left on plate, i.e., a man who has no girlfriend). Women changed from being the "sex that is named" to the "sex that names."

Let us look at some written examples that illustrate women's use of *ryūkōgo* and *wakamonogo*. From July through November 1996, *Asahi Shinbun's* Sunday edition featured a weekly column called "Wakamonogo," in which Yonekawa Akihiko gave specific examples, along with explanations of their meanings and usage. The following dialogue is taken from the July 27, 1996, column.

Midori: *Uchi no baito-saki no tenchō, tokku ni sanjū sugiten no ni mada dokushin nan ya de.*
"The store manager where I work part time is well over thirty, but he's still a bachelor."

Ayami: *Seikaku waruin?*
"Is his personality the problem?"

Midori: *Uun. Mitame ga nee . . .*
"Nah. His looks . . ."

Ayami: *Kawaisō ni, <u>Paseri-kun</u> yan.*
      "Poor thing! He's a 'Mr. Parsley.'"

It is important to note that both speakers in this conversation are women.

Joshi daisei kara mita rōjingo jiten (A Dictionary of the Language of Elderly People from the Perspective of Female University Students) (Yonekawa 1995), also written by Yonekawa, is compiled entirely from examples taken from conversations between elderly persons and their granddaughters, university students, who are using *ryūkōgo*, which is essentially a foreign language to older people. The following dialogue illustrates the communication gap.

Granddaughter:	*Obāchan, ano hito <u>batsuichi</u> ni nattan yatte.*
	"Grandma, they say that guy is now *Batsuichi.*"
Grandmother:	*Sore wa sugoi na.*
	"Really? That's great."
Granddaughter:	*Nan de sugoin?*
	"Great? Why?"
Grandmother:	*<u>Batsu</u>gun ni <u>ichi</u>ban nan yaro?*
	"You said he's 'first beyond compare,' right?"
Granddaughter:	*Chaute! Rikon shitan yatte!*
	"No, that's not what I meant! I said he got divorced!"
Grandmother:	*Hee, sonai iuun kai*
	"What do you know! Is that what you call it now?"
	(Yonekawa 1995, 16 [underlining by Endō])

Batsuichi, the term that the granddaughter uses, literally means "one x" or "one strike."

It seems that fashionable words are no longer disdained for their supposed vulgarity. Women today create and use new terms, which are then reported in the mass media and spread throughout society until even men come to use them.

NYŌBŌ-KOTOBA AND RYŪKŌGO— SIMILARITIES IN WORD FORMATION

Now, let us look at how *ryūkōgo* are formed and determine if the methods used to coin new words are similar in any way to those of *nyōbō-kotoba*. Here is a brief review of the word formation methods of *nyōbō-kotoba* as described in chapter 2.

(1) Addition of the honorific prefix *o-*
(2) Abbreviation of the original word
(3) Addition of *moji* to part of the original word

(4) Addition of *mono* to a word that is associated with the original word
(5) Referring to the word by its color, shape, or other
(6) Doubling one part of the original word or a word associated with it
(7) Using the native Japanese instead of the customary Chinese readings for the characters used to write the word.

Contemporary *wakamono-kotoba* uses many of the same word-formation techniques.

(1) Addition of the honorific prefix *o-* to the word or a shortened form of it
    o-keba < <u>*kebai*</u> *josei* "a garish woman"
    o-soro < *o-*<u>*soroi*</u> "a couple"
    o-taku < *zai*<u>*taku*</u> *shite asobu hito* "a loner who is obsessed with a hobby, such as computers or comic books"
    o-mizu< <u>*mizu*</u>*shōbai no hito* "a person who works in the bar and restaurant business"

In *nyōbō-kotoba*, the honorific prefix *o* was added to nouns denoting inanimate objects and to certain adjectives both to make the item referred to esthetically more pleasing and to make the speaker seem more refined. However, in *wakamono-kotoba*, the prefix *o* is used to create a group of words that refer to people and not things. Instead of giving the noun an elegant air, the *o-* prefix creates a noun with an entirely different meaning. For example, the addition of *o-* to a word such as *taku* "home" or *mizu* "water" creates the new lexical items *o-taku* and *o-mizu*, which refer to types of people, not the original inanimate objects.

(2) Abbreviation of the original word.

Nyōbō-kotoba frequently abbreviated long words. *Wakamono-kotoba* uses two methods of abbreviation.

(a) Words simply truncated at the beginning or end, as in *nyōbō-kotoba.*

pachi < *pachinko*	"pinball"
nabi < *nabigētā*	"navigator"
pashiri < *tsukaipashiri*	"to use throughout"
saten < *kissaten*	"coffee shop"

(b) Words elided in two or more places.

katekyō < *kateikyōshi*	"tutor"
Kimutaku < *Kimura Takuya*	(the name of a popular entertainer)
dotakyan < *dotanba de kyanseru*	"to cancel at the last moment"

103

yan'egu < yangu eguzekutibu   "young executive"
dame-moto < dame de motomoto   "nothing to lose"

A large percentage of words in *wakamomo-kotoba*, 21 percent of the total, according to Yonekawa (1996), fall into either of these two categories. We should note that not only single words are shortened in this way, but also sentences and phrases such as *kiyobuta < Kiyomizudera no butai kara tobioriru*, "jumping from [the ledge of] Kiyomizu Temple," i.e., "to take a leap in the dark, take a chance," or *ginkoi < Ginza no koi no monogatari*, "Ginza Love Story," the name of a popular song.

(3) Addition of *Moji* to part of the original word; and
(4) Addition of *mono*

While *nyōbō-kotoba* formed words by adding the suffix *moji*, modern-day *wakamono-kotoba* creates new words and nuances by adding *mono*, which may mean either "[tangible] thing" or "person," depending on which kanji is used to write it. Formerly, *mono* was used in circumlocutions that described some quality of an object so that *ao-mono* "green things" referred to vegetables, and *kuro-mono* "black thing" referred to cooking pots. The Noun + *mono* construction is still used in modern Japanese in such nonslang words as *horidashi-mono*, "something dug up, a find," or *namake-mono*, "lazy person," but in the modern colloquial language . . . *mono da* is used syntactically to imply that a state or condition is deserved or to be expected, as in *Sonna koto shitara hinshuku mono da*, "If you do that you deserve to be censured."

Mono is not always used as a suffix, as the following examples show. Adding *mono ga aru* to the end of a sentence imparts a sense of greater indecisiveness or ambiguity.

Hito mae de hanasu no wa chotto kihazukashii *mono ga atta*
"Speaking in front of people was a bit embarrassing."
Koko de wakareru no wa tsurai *mono ga aru*.
"It feels awful parting in this way."

The following are some suffixes used in contemporary colloquial expressions to refer to both men and women.

(a) The addition of *kun*, a title used by superiors to refer to subordinates or by both males and females to refer to young men or boys
Atomu-kun "Mr. Atom" (a man with few prospects after marriage)

Honmaru-kun "Mr. Dungeon," (a man who is an ideal
marriage partner)
Mitsugu-kun "Mr. Financial Support" (a man who gives
presents)
Asshī-kun "Mr. Feet" (a man with a car who is willing to
drive a woman around)
Kīpu-kun "Mr. Keep" (a man with whom a woman stays
friendly in case she is dropped by her true love)

(b) The addition of *-o,* a common suffix used in male names
Chara-o < chara-chara "jingle-jingle" (a flashy or superficial
young man)
Todo-o < todo "sea lion" (a young man who looks like a
walrus)
Femi-o (a young man who dresses somewhat like a woman,
although he is neither homosexual nor a transvestite)
Washi-o < washi "a form of 'I' used by older men" (a retired
man who has nothing to do but follow his wife around
all day)

(c) The addition of *chan,* a title used for small children or intimates
Ahiru-chan < ahiru "duck" (a student who has no grades
higher than "two" out of "five" on his or her report card;
"duck," because the shape of a duck resembles "2")
Uran-chan < uranai "doesn't sell" (a young woman who is not
seeking marriage)
Naru-chan "narcissist"

(d) The addition of the suffixes "-er" or "-ee" taken from the
English
Gucchā (someone who is fond of items with a Gucci label)
jimotī < jimoto "local" (someone from the local area)
chīmā< "team" (a young person who hangs around in the
area around Tokyo's Shibuya Station)
furītā < "free" (a young person who works at a series of
undemanding jobs instead of settling upon a career)

The following words formed from English elements refer to objects or ideas
instead of to people.

(e) The addition of the English "-ing" to native Japanese elements
shikatt-ingu < shika to "decisively" (ignore someone)
hamar-ingu < hamaru "be ensnared" (becoming engrossed
with something)

(f) The addition of the English suffix "-tic" to native Japanese
elements

okama-chikku < *okama* "slang word for homosexual male"
(appearing to be homosexual)
otome-chikku < *otome* "maiden" (maidenly)

The combination of new suffixes with other components is a word-formation method common to both past and present word coinage.

(5) An object or concept is referred to by one of the colors, shapes, or other qualities that characterize it.

    (a) Colors and shapes
        dāku "dark" gloomy; depressed
        ninjin-musume "carrot girl" a thin, suntanned girl with hair dyed red
        burakku "black" extremely depressed
        burū "blue" depressed

    (b) Associations
        Ita-san "Miss Board" a girl who has a chest that is as flat as a board
        sudare "bamboo screen" a hairstyle with bangs that curl under
        doshaburi "downpour" failing university-level courses
        nama-ashi "raw legs" the legs of a woman not wearing panty hose
        bākōdo "bar code" a combed-over hairstyle adopted by men trying to hide their baldness

Wakamonogo does not contain lexical items based on abstractions or literary devices such as the *nyōbō-kotoba* term *ashibiki* which plays on use of the word as a conventional epithet (*makura kotoba*) for *yamadori* "copper pheasant." However, it does include humorous expressions based on visual images, such as the aforementioned *sudare* or *bākōdo*.

(6) Reduplication, doubling one part of the original word or a word associated with it.
    ike-ike "brilliant, flamboyant, bold"
    uru-uru "sad; teary-eyed"
    gan-gan "extremely" (a word used for stress or emphasis)
    gero-gero (an interjection used to expressed an unpleasant feeling)
    gonyo-gonyo (an interjection used to laugh off or avoid something)
    saku-saku "quickly, promptly"
    shike-shike "to have a pall cast over an occasion"
    dasa-dasa "unseemly; ugly, unfashionable"

bari-bari "extreme; extremely"
pinpon-pinpon "correct, right on" (imitation of the bell on a
quiz show)
peke-peke "strange or bad in some way"
boke-boke "totally exhausted"
rabu-rabu "love-love, lovey-dovey."[1]

There are more examples, too numerous to mention. It is interesting to note that none of the reduplication expressions in *wakamono-kotoba*
contain nouns, while such expressions in *nyōbō-kotoba* are made up almost
exclusively of nouns. The reduplicated expressions used in *wakamonogo* are
formed exclusively from adverbs, adjectives and interjections that express
states, appearances, or emotions.

Thus far, we have examined the similarities in word formation methods between *nyōbō-kotoba* and *wakamono-kotoba*. Each enhances the sense of
group cohesion among its users, and both speech styles demonstrate clear
similarities in overall characteristics and share many of the same word- formation methods.

If *nyōbō-kotoba* and *wakamono-kotoba* share similar word formation
patterns, they should be held in similar esteem. On the contrary, they are
considered to be at opposite extremes, with *nyōbō-kotoba* viewed as refined
and elegant, and the language of young women today as rude and obscene.
Here I must point out that, on the one hand, *nyōbō-kotoba* is not completely
refined because it does contain vulgar items formed from abbreviations. On
the other hand, the fashionable vocabulary coined by contemporary young
women contains humorous words of good taste. One must look in detail at
the actual characteristics of the two speech styles instead of focusing on the
features that reinforce the commentator's prejudices.

Now, let us look at word-formation methods peculiar to contemporary *wakamono-kotoba*.

(1) The use of a prefix to express extremity and to add emphasis.
    (a) The addition of *chō*
        chō-nemui "super sleepy"
        chō-samui "super cold"
        chō-kowai "super frightening"
        chō-umai "super delicious"

Note that *chō* may be abbreviated to *cho* and the *i* in adjectives like *nemui* or
samui may be dropped to create forms such as *cho-nemu* or *cho-samu*.

    (b) The addition of *geki*
        geki-uma "extremely delicious"

geki-kara "extremely spicy"
geki-mukatsuku "extremely maddening"
(c) The addition of *mecha*
mecha-umai or *mechauma* "terribly delicious"
mecha-ii "terribly good"

Note that *mecha* may become *meccha* and also doubled to form *mechamecha*.

(d) The addition of *oni* "demon"
oni-muzukashii "difficult as hell"
oni-mazu "bad-tasting as hell"
(e) The addition of *sūpā* "super"
sūpā-sugoi "super great"
sūpā-yada "super yucky"
(f) The addition of *haipā* "hyper"
haipā-sugoi "hyperfantastic"
(g) The addition of *dera* an abbreviation of "deluxe"
dera-sugoi "deluxe fantastic"
dera-yasashii "deluxe nice"

There are cases when more than one of these prefixes are used together.

chō-urutora-sūpā-kakkoī "extremely, ultra, super good-looking"
chō-beri-ba < *chō beri badd)* "extremely very bad"
chō MM < *chō mukatsuk)* "extremely honestly maddening"

Excessive exaggeration is one characteristic of *wakamono-kotoba*. It seems that by the time an expression has gained some currency, it is already worn out and young people feel the need for an even more exaggerated expression. This results in a string of increasingly exaggerated expressions being formed.

(2) Puns are another favorite device
uri-futago a blend of *uri futatsu* "[as alike as] two bitter melons" and *futago* "twins" (people who look exactly alike)
shinguru beru a blend of *shinguru* "single" and "Jingle Bells" (a person who doesn't have a date on Christmas Eve)
(3) Rearrangement of syllables
gurasan < *sangurasu* "sunglasses"
shiime < *meshi* "rice, meal"
dachitomo < *tomodachi* "friend"
derumo ≤ *moderu* "fashion model"
waiha < *Hawaii* "Hawaii"

(4) Verbs are created from nouns by adding *ru*. (The standard Japanese equivalents, if any, are in parentheses.)

    kopi-ru (*kopii wo suru*) "to make copies"
    taku-ru (*takushii ni noru*) "to take a taxi"
    torabu-ru (*toraburu wo okosu; toraburu ga okiru*) "to make
    trouble; to have trouble"
    paniku-ru (*atama ga panikku ni naru*) "to be in a panic"
    paro-ru (*parodī ka suru*) "to make a parody of"

(5) The addition of *suru* "to do" to form verbs
    ettchi suru (*sekkusu suru*) "to have sex"
    ocha suru (*kissaten ni iku*) "to go to a tea shop"

(6) Modification of pronunciation in a manner reminiscent of
baby talk
    Urepii < *ureshii* "happy"
    Okapi < *okashii* "funny; strange"
    rappii < *rakkii* "lucky"
    dechū < *desu* (the copula)

(7) Rhyming puns are popular.
    sonna banana < *sonna baka na* "too strange to be true" + *banana*
    wakewakame < *wake wakaranai* "can't figure it out" plus
    wakame "a kind of seaweed"
    katte ni shirokuma < *katte ni shiro* "do as you please" +
    shirokuma ("polar bear")

In addition to the new lexical items described above, there are other modes of expression peculiar to *ryūkōgo*. Examples include intonation and accent such as the flattening of *kareshi*, "boyfriend" and *kanari*, "quite," rising intonation at the end of sentences, and the use of grammatical forms such as *-tte iu ka/ . . . tsuu ka*, "I mean," *to ka*, "and whatever," *. . . da shi*, "and, you know," *. . . tte kanji* "sort of like," and *. . . da yo ne*, it sure is, isn't it."

THE SOCIAL POSITIONING OF *RYŪKŌGO*

Yonekawa (1996) identifies four reasons for the growth in words coined by women:

(1) The breakdown of the value system that supported Japan's rapid economic growth until the late 1980s, when the so-called "bubble economy" collapsed, leading to open rejection of adult and male-centered societal values.

(2) Social advances in the 1980s that led to greater awareness of gender equality.

(3) Separating sex from love and marriage; this can be seen in the popularity of "love games" as one emblem of stylish city life promoted by women's magazines and other popular media; in these

media, men are viewed as "fashion accessories" for women.
(4) Aggressive marketing campaigns that targeted women through
the height of the bubble economy. Women are now pivotal to the
present consumption-oriented economy.

We have already discussed how women gained the power to coin
words. However, as noted above, we need also be aware that this cannot be
attributed solely to women's growing autonomy. Women were bombarded
with commercial appeals, cajoled, and used by players in the bubble economy, just like the jargon that was created at the time. While women began to
enjoy their newfound personal power, they were also targeted by merchants
who pursued them for their increased purchasing power. Big business and
the mass media have manipulated many and continue to do so.

In the 19 September 1996 edition of her column *Onna no gyakushū*
(Women's Counterattack) in the *Mainichi Shinbun*, Kobayashi Yoko, colum-
nist for the *Mainichi Shinbun*, angrily reports the following incident involv-
ing two junior high school students and the camera crew of a TV program:

> "So, tell me the abbreviations you use when sending mes-
> sages to your *beru-tomo*" (<*Pokketto beru tomodachi:* "pager pals").
> Speaking affected *wakamonogo* the interviewer hands the mike
> over to the students.
> "What? Abbreviations? You want me to say *choberiba* and
> stuff, right?"
> "Or *barimuka* and . . ."
> "Yeh, that's it. That's great. . . ."
> The reporter was openly egging them on and the students
> played along with him.
> Kobayashi continues, "I think it is high time for the mass me-
> dia to stop chasing after junior and senior high school students.
> They should start putting the spotlight back on real adults."

We must realize that the peculiar meanings and new functions of
coined words are not the only reason that women receive extensive attention and acknowledgment as users of *ryūkōgo*. It goes much deeper than
that.

With respect to the overall significance of *wakamonogo*, Yonekawa
states that it is "a *playful language* form [italics Yonekawa] created by free
spirits who want to liberate themselves from set standards" and that it is a
form of *karui nori*, a manifestation of a "carefree and easy culture," used for
amusement and as a means to promote conversation.

As stated above, young people, especially young women, use *ryūkōgo* and *wakamonogo* in order to feel "carefree and easy." They seem to be

singing the joys of the springtime of their lives. Unfortunately, though, this may be the last time in their lives when they are truly able to shine. Perhaps they somehow know that a darker period, one filled with oppression and discrimination, awaits them as women. Let's hope this is not so.

Whatever the case may be, women of earlier generations might envy the way in which young women today enjoy word-play, word associations, creating pastiches of existing expressions, coining abbreviations, and adding amusing endings to form new words to share among their friends. Never before have women had the freedom to present their thoughts and feelings to the world in words of their own. It is marvelous to live through the first time in Japanese history when women are able to enjoy such freedom. I feel compassion for the women who went before us—women controlled by a male-dominated society and forced to be unfailingly polite in their language.

It is impossible for young Japanese women to reform the structure of the adult society that awaits them by remaining cocooned in their own world with *ryūkōgo*. Even so, I place my hopes in the young women of Japan and trust that as they mature, they will turn their boundless energy to creating a new "adult" language, too. I am hopeful that they will now turn their energies to coining new words that promise a better relationship between the sexes, instead of expressions that slight men such as *Asshī-kun* and *Mitsugu-kun*.

We have reviewed and discussed the path that Japanese women's language followed in its evolution from ancient times to the present day. And we can finally offer a conclusive answer to my original question of whether "women's language" can be found in the earliest attested forms of Japanese. The answer is, no. A distinctive women's language has not always existed.

There is a tendency to accept without question as "tradition" or "culture" phenomena that existed before we were born. It seems reasonable to assume that women have spoken "women's language" since antiquity. However, now that we realize that "women's language" was created after the medieval period, we must free ourselves from this subjective impression.

Japanese women have been forced to use language contrary to their true feelings. Although many women I know dislike calling their husband *shujin* "master" because it implies they are his slave, they continue to use the word for fear of being labeled "haughty" or "strong-willed." Many young women who refer to themselves as *boku* in junior high school change from *boku* to *watashi* because their parents and teachers scold them or because they give in to pressure from their surroundings.

It is a miserable feeling to have to alter one's speech and refrain from using the words that most accurately express one's feelings in order to avoid offending society. Young women now are not shackled by the "women's language" of the past, and have begun to claim a genderless, relaxed language style. We may soon see the day when they can express their ideas and emotions in whatever speech style they choose.

NOTE

1. Also used between same-sex couples.

BIBLIOGRAPHY

[For Japanese works, the place of publication
is Tokyo unless otherwise noted.]

FNF1-Fukkoku Nihon no fujin zasshi 1 (Ōzorasha)
—*Fujin kyōiku zasshi* 1986
—*Jokan* 1986
—*Joken* 1986
—*Nihon no jogaku* 1986

FNF3-Fukkoku Nihon no fujin zasshi 3 (Ōzorasha)
—*Fujinkai* 1986
—*Fujin kurabu* 1986
—*Fujin sekai* 1986

KBSJ-Kinsei bungei shūsho 10 (Kokusho kankōkai)
—*Satonamari* 1911.

NKBJH-Nihon kyōiku bunko-Jokun hen (Nihon tosho sentā)
—*Menoto no fumi* 1910.
—*Menoto no sōshi* 1910.
—*Mi no katami* 1910.

NKBT-Nihon koten bungaku taikei (Iwanami shoten)
—*Chikamatsu jōruri shū jō* 83, 1958.
—*Heike monogatari Jō* 32, 1959.
—*Heike monogatari Ge* 33, 1960.
—*Hōjōki—Tsurezuregusa* 30, 1957.
—*Kabuki kyakuhon shū jō* 53, 1960.
—*Kana hogo shu* 83, 1964.
—*Konjaku monogatari shū* 4, 1962.
—*Konjaku monogatari shū* 5, 1963.
—*Otogizōshi* 38, 1958.
—*Tsuma kagami* 83, 1964.

—*Ukiyo buro* 63, 1967.

NKTJY-Nihon kyōkasho taikei joshi yō (Kōdansha)
—*Onna dōshi kyō* 1973.
—*Shinsen onna yamato daigaku* 1973.

NKTKS-Nihon kyōkasho taikei kindaihen shūshin 2 (Kōdansha)
—*Jinjō shōgaku shūshin sho* 1962
—*Shinpen shūshin sho* 1962
—*Shōgaku sahō sho* 1962
—*Shōgaku shūshin kun* 1962
—*Shōgaku shūshin sho* 1962

OS-Onna shisho (Yūhōdō)
—*Jokai* 1928.
—*Naikun* 1928.

SNK-Shinchō Nihon kotenshūsei (Shinchōsha)
—*Hōjōki Hosshin shū* 1976.
—*Kokonchomonjū* 1983.

Abe Hideko. 2001. "Kuia gengo kara mita 'onna-rashii' kotoba." In *Onna to kotoba—onna wa kawatta ka Nihongo wa kawatta ka*, pp. 217–27. Edited by Endō Orie. Akashi shoten.
_____. 2004. "Lesbian Bar Talk in Shinjyuku, Tokyo." In *Japanese Language, Gender, and Ideology: Cultural Models and Real People*, pp. 205–21. Edited by Okamoto Shigeko and Janet S. Shibamoto Smith. New York: Oxford University Press.
Abe Keiko. 1990. "Dēta ni miru gendai no onna kotoba no seitai." *Gekkan Nihongo*, vol. 3, no. 2, pp. 7–11.
Agency for Cultural Affairs. 1995. *Kokugo ni kan suru seron chōsa*. National Language Section, Culture Department, Agency for Cultural Affairs.
Ashida Enosuke. 1973. *Tsuzurikata kyōjuhō, Tsuzurikata kyōiku ni kan suru kyōshi no shūyō*. Tamagawa daigaku shuppanbu.
"Atarashii onnarashisa" (A new femininity). *Fujin kōron* (Women's public opinions), July, 1948.
Bandō Tamasaburō. 1994a. "Tamasaburō no sekai." *Asahi shinbun*, May 9.
_____. 1994b. "Tamasaburō no sekai." *Asahi shinbun*, May 11.
Beppu Keiko, ed. 1989. *Bungaku shakai ni okeru josei to gengo*. Yumi shobō.
Cameron, Deborah. 1985. *Feminism and Linguistic Theory*. New York: Macmillan. Translated into Japanese by Nakamura Momoko as *Feminizu-*

mu to gengoriron. Keisō shobō, 1990.

Cherry, Kittredge. 1987. *Womansword: What Japanese Words Say about Women.* Kodansha International. Translated into Japanese by Kurihara Yōko and Nakanishi Kiyomi as *Nihongo wa onna wo dō hyōgen shite kita ka.* Fukutake shoten, 1990.

Coates, Jennifer. 1986. *Women, Men and Language: A Sociolinguistic Account of Sex Differences in Languages.* London and New York: Longman. Translated into Japanese by Yoshida Masaharu as *Onna to otoko to kotoba—Joseigo no shakaigengogakuteki kenkyūhō.* Kenkyūsha, 1990.

Dan Michiko. 1943. *Josei to kotoba.* Sakuragi shobō.

Endō Motoo. 1946. *Josei bunkashi.* Shinfu shoten.

Endō Orie. 1980. "Josei wo arawasu kotoba." *Kotoba*, vol. 1, pp. 19–54.

_____. 1981. "Jisho ni miru josei—kokugo jiten kyōdō kenkyū: otoko ga tsuku kotoba, onna ga tsuku kotoba." *Kotoba*, vol. 2, pp. 25–40.

_____. 1982. "Jisho to shinbun ni miru dansei to josei." *Kotoba*, vol. 3, pp. 1–20.

_____. 1983. "Josei wo arawasu kotoba (2): Meiji nijū nendai wo chūshin ni." *Kotoba*, vol. 4, pp. 1–27.

_____. 1984. "Kokugo jisho kenkyū: onna no me de mita *Kōjien.*" *Kotoba*, vol. 5, pp. 1–19.

_____. 1985. "Haigūsha wo yobu kotoba: 'shujin' wo megutte." *Kotoba*, vol. 6, pp. 29–49.

_____. 1986. "Haigusha wo yobu kotoba (2): Otto kara tsuma wo." *Kotoba*, vol. 7, pp. 1–21.

_____. 1987. *Ki ni naru kotoba: Nihongo saikentō.* Nan'undō.

_____. 1989. "Josei no hanashikotoba to wa: Terebi no intabyū bangumi kara." *Kotoba*, vol. 10, pp. 18–35.

_____. 1990a. "Dansei no hanashikotoba: Josei no hanashikotoba to hikaku shite." *Kotoba*, vol. 11, pp. 61–85.

_____. 1990b. "Onna rashii Nihongo wo oshieru-beki ka?" *Gekkan Nihongo*, vol. 3, no. 2, pp. 12–13.

_____. 1991a. "Kotoba to josei." *Kokubungaku: kaishaku to kanshō*, vol. 56, no. 7, pp. 28–37.

_____. 1991b. "Manga ni miru joshi chūkōsei no hanashikotoba: Bunmatsu kara mita manga no joshi chūkōsei no hanashikotoba." *Kotoba*, vol. 12, pp. 1–8, 9–25.

_____. 1992a. "Kyōdō kenkyū, josei no kotoba to sedai: Josei no gengo shiyō, gengo-kan to sedai-sa." *Kotoba*, vol. 13, pp. 79–97.

_____, ed. 1992b. *Josei no yobikata daikenkyū: Gyaru kara obasan made.* Sanseidō.

_____. 1993a. "Kyōdō kenkyū, josei no kotoba to sedai II: (1) Hanashikotoba no naka no kakujoshi." *Kotoba*, vol. 14, pp. 54–69.

_____. 1993b. "Sexism in Japanese Language Dictionaries." *Japan Quarterly* (October-November), pp. 395–98.

_____. 1994a. "Kyōdō kenkyū: Shokuba ni okeru josei no hanashikotoba, sono 2, shiyō goshu to atarashii kotoba no yōhō." *Kotoba,* vol. 15, pp. 114–34.

_____. 1994b. "Manga no hanashikotoba." *Kokubungaku, kaishaku to kanshō,* vol. 59, no. 1, pp. 105–18.

_____. 1994c. "Wakai josei no kotoba: Ronpyō de tsuzuru sono Shōwa-shi." *Nihongogaku,* vol. 13, no. 11, pp. 19–32.

_____. 1995a. "Aspects of Sexism in Language." In *Japanese Women: New Feminist Perspectives on the Past, Present, and Future,* pp. 29–42. Edited by Kumiko Fujimura-Fanselow and Atsuko Kameda. The Feminist Press at the City University of New York.

_____. 1995b. "Josei to moji: Chūgoku onna moji ga shisa suru mono." In *Onna to otoko no jikū I: hime to hiko no jidai,* pp. 439–71. Edited by Kōno Nobuko. Fujiwara shoten.

_____. 1995c (with Yabe Hiroko). "Kyōdō kenkyū: Shokuba ni okeru josei no hanashikotoba, sono 3: Hanashikotoba ni tokuchōteki na go no atarashii yōhō to sedai-sa." *Kotoba,* vol. 16, pp. 114–27.

_____. 1995d. "Joseigo nanka kietatte ii." *Kyaria gaidansu,* March. pp. 40–50.

_____. 1996. "Meiji jidai no 'Joseigaku': Yamaguchi Kotarō no josei-kan to yōgo 'joseigaku.'" *Kotoba,* vol. 17, pp. 102–13.

_____. 1997a. *Onna no kotoba no bunka-shi.* Gakuyō shobō.

_____. 1997b. "Shokuba no keigo no ima." In *Josei no kotoba: Shokuba hen,* pp. 83–111. Edited by Gendai Nihongo Kenkyūkai. Hitsuji shobō.

_____. 1998a. *Ki ni narimasu, kono "kotoba."* Shōgakkan.

_____. 1998b. "Kokugo jiten ni miru josei e no henken, keishi." In *Kotoba ni miru "josei,"* pp. 142–85. Edited by Tōkyō Josei Zaidan. Kureyon hausu.

_____. 1998c. "Tōkyō no josei no kotoba no ima." *Gengo,* vol. 27, no. 1, pp. 76–81.

_____. 1998d (with Ozaki Yoshimitsu). "Josei no kotoba no hensen." *Nihongogaku,* vol. 17, no. 5, pp. 56–79.

_____. 1999. "Kōreisha no hanashikata wa osokute wakarinikui ka: Hanashikotoba no sedai-sa wo miru kokoromi." *Kotoba,* vol. 20, pp. 83–94.

_____. 2000. "Ninki dorama no hanashikotoba ni miru seisa: TV dorama *Byūtifuru Raifu* no moji-ka shiryō kara." *Kotoba,* vol. 21, pp. 13–23.

_____, ed. 2001. *Onna to kotoba—Onna wa kawatta ka, Nihongo wa kawatta ka.* Akashi shoten.

_____. 2002a. *Chūgoku onnamoji kenkyū.* Meiji shoin.

_____. 2002b. "'Joseigo' to iu shisō." *Kotoba,* vol. 23, pp. 40–58.

_____. 2002c. "Dansei no kotoba no bunmatsu." In *Dansei no kotoba: Shokuba hen*, pp. 33–45. Edited by Gendai Nihongo Kenkyūkai. Hitsuji shobō.

———. 2003. "Otoko wa donari, onna wa donarareru—Shinbun tōshoshū 'Otōsan, donaranaide' to shinbunkiji kensaku dēta kara." *Kotoba*, vol. 24, pp. 26–42.

——— et al. 2004a. "Senjichū no hanashikotoba no gaikan." In *Senjichū no hanasikotoba—rajio dorama daihon kara*, pp. 27–64. Hitsuji shobō.

——— et al. 2004b. "'Tennō' ni kan suru yōgo." In *Senjichū no hanasikotoba—rajio dorama daihon kara*, pp. 65–81. Hitsuji shobō.

——— et al. 2004c. "Ninshōshi no tukawarekata." In *Senjichū no hanasikotoba—rajio dorama daihon kara*, pp. 83–97. Hitsuji shobō.

——— et al. 2004d. "Daihon no egaku jyoseitachi." In *Senjichū no hanasikotoba—rajio dorama daihon kara*, pp. 195–228. Hitsuji shobō.

———. 2005. "Sabetsugo, fukaigo no 60-nen." In *Hyōgen to buntai*. pp. 437–55. Edited by Nakamura Akira et al. Meiji shoin.

"Fujinkai." Fukkoku Nihon no fujin zasshi, vol. 3. Ōzorasha, 1986.

"Fujin kurabu." Fukkoku Nihon no fujin zasshi, vol. 3. Ōzorasha, 1986.

"Fujin kyōiku zasshi." Fukkoku Nihon no fujin zasshi, vol. 1. Ōzorasha, 1986.

"Fujin sekai" (Women's world). *Fukkoku Nihon no fujin zasshi*, vol. 3. Ōzorasha, 1986.

Fukuchi Shigetaka. 1963. *Kindai Nihon no josei-shi*. Sekkasha.

Fukuda Mayumi. 1993. *"Shujin" to iu kotoba*. Akashi shoten.

Fukuda Sadayoshi. 1973. "Onna no ronri, otoko no ronri." *Gengo seikatsu* 262, pp. 14–22.

Furuya Tsunatake. 1946. "Utsukushii kotoba." *Fujin kōron* (April), pp. 33–35.

Gendai Nihongo Kenkyūkai, ed. 1994. *Shokuba ni okeru hanashikotoba: shizen danwa no moji-ka shiryō ni motozuite*. Tōkyō Josei Zaidan hōjin 1993 nendo Josei kenkyū hōkokusho.

———. 1997. *Josei no kotoba: Shokuba hen*. Hitsuji shobō.

———, ed. 2002. *Dansei no kotoba: Shokuba hen*. Hitsuji shobō.

Gendai yōgo no kiso chishiki 1986 (Basic knowledge about contemporary terms 1986). Jiyū kokuminsha, 1986.

Gotō Toshio. 1986. *Man'yōshū seiritsu shinron*. Ōfūsha.

Hachiya Kiyoto. 1988. "Kanji to isō." In *Kanji kōza 4: Kanji to kana*, pp. 14–43. Edited by Satō Kiyoji. Meiji shoin.

Hamada Atsushi. 1946. *Kodai nihongo*. Ōyashima shuppan.

Han Son Hi. 1991. "Manga ni miru joshi chūkōsei no hanashikotoba: Shukuyakukei ni tsuite." *Kotoba*, vol. 12, pp. 72–83.

———. 1994. "Kankoku de wa otto wo dō yobu ka?" *Kotoba*, vol. 15, pp. 70–88.

Hasegawa Nyozekan. 1943. *Kotoba to bunka*. Chūō kōronsha.

Hattori Yoshika. 1954. "Nyōbō kotoba." In *Kotoba no kenkyūshitsu: kotoba no yurai*, pp. 108–21. Kōdansha.

Hayashi Dai, et al. 1988. *Nihongo hyakka daijiten.* Taishūkan.

Hida Yoshibumi. 1975. "Gendai Nihongo no keisei." In *Shin Nihongo kōza 4: Nihongo no rekishi,* pp. 227–59. Edited by Iwabuchi Etsutarō and Hida Yoshibumi. Chōbunsha.

Hirai Masao. 1960. "Shitsurei ni naranai kotoba." In *Hen na kotoba, tadashii kotoba,* pp. 148–52. Kadokawa shoten.

Hiratsuka Raichō. 1911. "Genshi josei wa taiyō de atta." *Seitō.*

Hirota Masaki. 1982. "Bunmei kaika to josei kaihōron." In *Nihon joseishi 4: kindai,* edited by Joseishi sōgō kenkyū kai. Tōdai shuppankai.

Hisamatsu Sen'ichi. 1962. "Man'yōshū," In *Waka bungaku daijiten.* Meiji shoin.

Honda Akiko. 1995. "Jitsurei no mirareru Nihongo no danjo-sa: Denwa ni yoru atarashii dōsei dōshi no shiteki na kaiwa no bunseki kara." *Kotoba,* vol. 16, pp. 69–83.

_____. 2001. "Doko ga chigau, onna no ko no kotoba to otoko no ko no ko-toba." In *Onna to kotoba—onna wa kawatta ka Nihongo wa kawatta ka,* pp. 138–44. Edited by Endō Orie. Akashi shoten.

Hongō Akemi. 1981. "Jisho ni miru josei: Kokugo jiten kyōdō kenkyū, koku-go jiten no yōrei ni arawareru 'Otoko wo arawasu kotoba,' 'Onna wo arawasu kotoba.'" *Kotoba,* vol. 2, pp. 41–49.

Hori Motoko. 1983. "Keigo no sokutei ni kansuru kokoromi (1): Danjo-sa no hikaku kara." *Tsudajuku Daigaku kiyō,* vol. 15, pp. 179–204.

_____. 2000. "Shakai no henka to gengo no henka." In *Gendai wakamono ko-toba no chōryū: Kyori wo okanai wakamonotachi,* pp. 3–24. Daigaku Eigo Kyōiku Gakkai Chūbu Shibu Taigū Hyōgen Kenkyū Kai.

Horii Reiichi. 1989. "Dansei no kotoba to josei no kotoba." In *Kōza Nihongo to Nihongo kyōiku,* vol. 1, pp. 241–58. Edited by Miyaji Yutaka. Meiji shoin.

_____. 1990. *Onna no kotoba.* Meiji shoin.

_____. 1992. *Hataraku josei no kotoba.* Meiji shoin.

Hosaka Kazushi. 1995. "Kono hito no iki." *Bungei shunjū,* September.

Hoshina Kōichi. 1936. *"Fujin no kotoba to kodomo no kotoba."* In *Kokugo to Nihongo seishin.* Jitsugyō no Nihonsha.

Ide Risako. 1998 (with Terada Tomomi). "The Historical Origins of Japanese Women's Speech: From the Secluded Worlds of 'Court Ladies' and 'Play Ladies.'" *International Journal of Society and Languages* 129, pp. 139–56.

Ide Sachiko. 1979. *Onna no kotoba, otoko no kotoba.* Nihon keizai tsūshinsha.

_____. 1980. "Eigo to Nihongo no naka no joseigo." *Gekkan kotoba,* vol. 3, no. 12, pp. 2–7.

_____. 1981. "Onna no bunshō to onna-rashisa: Kimura Harumi no buntai no kēsu sutadī." In *Kotoba no shakaisei,* pp. 61–70. Edited by Hori Motoko and F.C. Peng. Bunka hyōron shuppan.

_____. 1982. "Taigū hyōgen to danjo-sa no hikaku." In *Nichiei hikaku go kōza,* pp. 107–9. Taishūkan shoten.

_____. 1983. "Onna rashisa no gengogaku: Naze onna wa joseigo wo tsukau no ka?" In *Kōza Nihongo no hyōgen 3,* pp. 174–93. Chikuma shobō.

_____. 1986. "Gengo kōdō no toraekata: Danjo-sa kenkyū no rironteki moderu." In *Ōyō gengogaku kōza 2: Gaikokugo to Nihongo,* pp. 115–34. Edited by Hayashi Shirō. Meiji shoin.

_____. 1992 (with Inoue Miyako). "Josei kotoba ni miru aidentitī: Shakai no josei no baai." *Gengo,* vol. 21, no. 10, pp. 46–47.

_____, ed. 1993. "Sekai no joseigo, Nihon no joseigo—joseigo kenkyū no shintenkai wo motomete." *Nihongogaku* (special extra issue for May).

_____ and Naomi Hanaoka McGloin, eds. 1990. *Aspects of Japanese Women's Language.* Kuroshio.

Igeta Ryoji. 1982. "Meiji Minpō to josei no kenri." In *Nihon joseishi 4: kindai,* edited by Joseishi sōgō kenkyū kai. Tōdai shuppankai.

Ikeda Yasaburō. 1966a. "'O' no samazama." *Fujin kōron* (November), pp. 210–11.

_____. 1966b. "Utsukushii kotoba." *Fujin kōron* (July), pp. 208–9.

Inagaki Yoshihiko. 1999. *Heisei shingo x ryūkōgo jiten.* Kōdansha.

Inoguchi Yūichi. 1974 (with Horii Reiichi). *Gosho kotoba.* Yūzankaku.

Inoue Yōsui. 1994. *Mainichi shinbun* (November 19).

Ishiguro Yoshimi. 1943. "Joseigo no hattatsu." In *Utsukushii Nihongo,* pp. 222–36. Kōfūkan.

Ishii Shōji. 1941. "Chūtō gakkō no kokugo kyōiku." In *Nihongo bunka kōza dai 3 kan kokugo kyōiku hen,* pp. 15–70. Asahi shinbunsha.

Ishino Hiroshi. 1980. "Nihongo wa midarete iru ka?" In *Nihonjin to hanashi-kotoba.* Nihon hōsō shuppan kyōkai.

_____. 1991 (with Yasuhira Minako). "Nihonjin no kotoba ishiki to kore kara no Nihongo." In *NHK Hōsō bunka kenkyūjo nenpō,* pp. 83–113. NHK Hōsō Bunka Kenkyūjo.

Itami Sueo. 1988. *Man'yōshū seiritsu shinkō.* Kasama shoin.

"Jinjō shōgaku shūshin sho." Nihon kyōkasho taikei kindaihen 2 shūshin 2. Kōdansha, 1962.

"Jogaku shinshi." Fukkoku Nihon no fujin zasshi, vol. 1. Ōzorasha, 1986.

"Joken." Fukkoku Nihon no fujin zasshi, vol. 1. Ōzorasha, 1986.

"Josei no hanashi kotoba—terebi no intabyū bangumi kara." In *Kotoba,* vol. 10. Gendai Nihongo Kenkyūkai, 1989.

Joseishi Sōgō Kenkyūkai, ed. 1983. *Nihon joseishi 4: Kindai.* Tōdai shuppankai.

Jugaku Akiko. 1964a. "Onna ga kakeba, onna-rashiku naru ka?" *Gengo seikatsu* 159, pp. 17–32.

_____. 1964b. "Joseigo to keigo." *Kokubungaku,* vol. 11, no. 8, pp. 143–48.

_____. 1975. "Joseigo 50-nen." *Gengo seikatsu* 282, pp. 27–33.

_____. 1978. "Joseigo ni totte no Shōwa." In *Kotoba no Shōwa-shi*. Edited by Ōishi Hatsutarō et al. Asahi sensho.

_____. 1979. *Nihongo to onna* (Iwanami shinsho). Iwanami shoten.

_____. 1982. "Onna-rashisa to Nihongo." In *Nihongo to Nihonjin* pp. 215–65. Kōdansha.

_____. 1985. "Joseigo no 60-nen." *Gengo*, vol. 14, no.1, pp. 102–3.

_____. 1991. "Kotoba no kenkyū to josei." *Kokubungaku kaishaku to kanshō*, vol. 56, no. 7.

_____. 1995. "Kotowaza to joseishi." In *Onna to otoko no jikū IV: Ranjuku suru onna to otoko*, pp. 6–12. Edited by Fukuda Mitsuko. Fujiwara shoten.

Kaihara Tōru. 1996. *Nihonshi shohyakka "gakkō."* Tōkyōdō shuppansha.

Kanai Yoshiko, ed. 1997. *Media to josei no jinken*. Kanagawa Josei Sentā.

Kanamaru Fumi. 1993. "Ninshō daimeishi, koshō." *Nihongogaku* (special extra issue for May), pp. 109–19.

Kasuga Seiji. 1933. "Kana hattatsu-shi josetsu." In *Iwanami kōza Nihon bungaku*, pp. 1–94. Iwanami shoten.

Katō Akihiko et al., eds. 1989. *Nihongo gaisetsu* (An outline of the Japanese language). Ōfūsha.

Kawaguchi Yōko. 1987. "Majiriau danjo no kotoba: Jittai chōsa ni yoru genjō." *Gengo seikatsu* 429, pp. 34–39.

Keene, Donald, trans. 1967. *Essays in Idleness: The Tsurezuregusa of Kenkō*. New York: Columbia University Press.

Kikuzawa Sueo. 1929. "Fujin no kotoba no tokuchō ni tsuite." *Kokugo kyōiku* (March), pp. 66–75.

_____. 1933. "Kokugo isōron." In *Kokugo kagaku kōza III: Kokugogaku*, pp. 3–67. Meiji shoin.

_____. 1940. "Kokugo to kokuminsei" (National language and national character). In *Nihon seishin no senmei*, pp. 230–87. Shūbunkan.

Kindaichi Haruhiko. 1988. *Nihongo jo* (Iwanami shinsho). Iwanami shoten.

Kindaichi Kyōsuke. 1942. *"Joseigo to keigo."* In *Kokugo kenkyū*. Yagumo shorin.

Kinsei Bungaku Shoshi Kenkyūkai, ed. 1981. *Onna chōhōki*. Benseisha.

Kobayashi Chigusa. 1996. "Josei no ishiki to joseigo no keisei: nyōbō kotoba wo chūshin ni." In *Onna to otoko no jikū III: Onna to otoko no midare*, pp. 293–336. Edited by Okano Haruko. Fujiwara shoten.

Kobayashi Mieko. 1981. "Jisho ni miru josei: kokugo jiten kyōdō kenkyū: kokugo jiten ni miru otoko no kōi, onna no kōi." *Kotoba*, vol. 2, pp. 3–13.

_____. 1991. "Manga ni miru joshi kōkōsei no hanashikotoba: Jishōshi, taishōshi oyobi keigo hyōgen ni tsuite." *Kotoba*, vol. 12, pp. 26–59.

_____. 1992. "(Kyōdō kenkyū: Josei no kotoba to sedai) Shiryō: Josei no kotoba to sedai: Suzuki-san ikka." *Kotoba,* vol. 13, pp. 119–93.

_____. 1993a. "(Kyōdō kenkyū: Josei no kotoba to sedai II) (4) Zadan ni okeru wadai no tenkan." *Kotoba,* vol. 14, pp. 38–53.

_____. 1993b. "Sedai to joseigo: wakai josei no 'chūseika' ni tsuite." *Nihongogaku* (special extra issue for May), pp. 181–92.

_____. 1994. "Jirei kenkyū: Joshi kōkōsei no zatsudan." *Kotoba,* vol. 15, pp. 98–111.

_____. 1995. "Bunmatsu keishiki ni miru joshi kōkōsei no kaiwa kanri." *Kotoba,* vol. 16, pp. 35–51.

_____. 1998. "Otoko wa hontō ni o-shaberi ka?" *Kotoba,* vol. 19, pp. 128–37.

_____. 2003. "Shokuba ni okeru meirei—irai hyōgen." *Kotoba,* vol. 24, pp. 13–25.

Kōjien. 5th ed. Iwanami shoten, 1998.

Komai Gasei. 1951. *Kana no rekishi.* Nishhin shobō.

Komatsu Shigemi. 1968. *Kana* (Iwanami shinsho). Iwanami shoten.

Komatsu Hisao. 1987. "*Ukiyo-buro* ni okeru josei no ninshō to kaisō." In *Kindaigo kenkyū,* vol. 7, pp. 403–19. Musashino shoin.

Kōno Yūko. 1991. *Gendai tanka bunko Kōno Yūko kashū.* Sunakoya shobō.

"Kotoba no seisa sarani chiisaku." 1994. *Yomiuru shinbun,* October 14.

Kotoba to Onna wo Kangaeru Kai, eds. 1985. *Kokugo jiten ni miru josei sabetsu.* San'ichi shobō.

Koyano Tetsuo. 1994. "Joshi daisei no kyanpasu-kotoba." *Nihongogaku,* vol. 13, no. 10, pp. 45–53.

_____. 2000. "Hangyaku suru josei-kotoba no jendā." In *Jendā-gaku wo manabu hito no tame ni,* pp. 146–57. Sekai shisōsha.

Kōyō zenshū, vol. 10. Iwanami shoten, 1993.

Kōza Nihongo. Ōtsuki shoten, 1955.

Kugimoto Hisaharu. 1952. "Josei no kotoba." In *Gendai no Nihongo,* pp. 24–26. Kokin shoin.

Kunida Yuriko. 1964. *Nyōbō kotoba no kenkyū.* Kazama shobō.

_____. 1977. *Nyōbō kotoba no kenkyū: zoku hen.* Kazama shobō.

_____. 1984. "Keigo to joseigo." In *Gendai hōgengaku no kadai* 3. Edited by Hirayama Teruo Hakushi Koki Kinenkai. Meiji shoin.

Lakoff, Robin. 1975. *Language and Women's Place.* New York: Harper and Row. Translated into Japanese by Katsue Akiba Reynolds as *Gengo to sei—Eigo ni okeru onna no tii.* Yūshindō, 1990.

Maeda Tomiyoshi. 1973. "Josei no gengo seikatsu-shi." *Gengo seikatsu* 262, pp. 23–33.

_____. 1984. "Josei no rekishi to kotoba." *Gengo seikatsu* 387, pp. 22–30.

Mainichi shinbun, March 12, 1994.

Mainichi shinbun, April 23, 1996.

Mashimo Saburō. 1942. "Joseigo no seimei: moji-kotoba ni tsuite." In *Gendai Nihongo no kenkyū*, pp. 171–96. Hakusuisha.

———. 1948. *Fujingo no kenkyū*. Tōa shuppansha.

———. 1966. *Yūrigo no kenkyū*. Tōkyōdō shuppan.

———. 1967. *Joseigo jiten*. Tōkyōdō shuppan.

Masubuchi Tsunekichi, ed. 1981. *Kōgo kyōikushi shiryō 5, Kyōiku kateishi*. Tōkyōhōi shuppansha.

Matsumoto Yoshiko. 2004. "Alternative Femininity: Personae of Middle-aged Mothers." In *Japanese Language, Gender, and Ideology: Cultural Models and Real People*, pp. 240–55. Edited by Okamoto Shigeko and Janet S. Shibamoto Smith. New York: Oxford University Press.

McCullough, Helen Craig, trans. 1988. *The Tale of the Heike*. Stanford University Press.

McGloin, Naomi Hanaoka, and Ide Sachiko, eds. 1990. *Aspects of Japanese Women's Language*. Kuroshio.

Misesu Fujin kōron kenkyūkai. 1953. "Josei wa utsukushiku." *Fujin kōron*, March.

Mitsui Akiko. 1992. "Kyōdō kenkyū, josei no kotoba to sedai: Hanashi kotoba no sedai-sa: shūjoshi to fukushi wo chūshin ni." *Kotoba*, vol. 13, pp. 98–104.

Miyaji Yutaka. 1957. "Josei no nichijōgo." *Izumi*, vol. 2, no. 12, pp. 25–27.

Mogami Katsuya. 1986. "Hataraku josei no kotoba no ishiki." In *Hōsō kenkyū to chōsa*, no. 11, pp. 14–23. Nihon Hōsō shuppan kyōkai.

———. 1988. "'Josei no jidai' no kotoba ishiki." In *Hōsō kenkyū to chōsa*, no. 12, pp. 18–25. Nihon Hōsō shuppan kyōkai.

Mori Senzō. 1969. *Meiji Tōkyō itsubun-shi*. Tōyō Bunko 135. Heibonsha.

Morino Muneaki. 1975. *Ōchō no kizoku shakai no josei no gengo*. Yūseidō.

———. 1991. "Joseigo no rekishi." In *Kōza Nihongo to Nihongo kyōiku 10*, pp. 225–48. Edited by Tsujimura Toshiki. Meiji shoin.

Morita Tama. 1943. *Fujin tokuhon*, Seikatsusha.

Morita Yoshiyuki. 1991. "Goi genshō wo meguru danjo-sa." *Kokubungaku: kaishaku to kanshō*, vol. 56, no. 7, pp. 65–70.

Morris, Ivan, trans. 1967. *The Pillow Book of Sei Shōnagon*. New York: Columbia University Press.

Mozume Takakazu. 1922. "Makura no sōshi." In *Murasaki Shikibu nikki, Izumi Shikibu nikki, Sarashina nikki, Izayoi nikki, Makura no sōshi, Hōjōki, Tsurezuregusa*. Nihon bungaku sōsho kankōkai.

Murakami Shizuto. 1915. *Sato uguisu* (Warbler in the quarters). Ninjōbon kankōkai.

———, ed. 1915. *Shunshoku yuki no ume* (Spring views, a plum tree in snow). Ninjōbon kankōkai.

Muramatsu Chieko. 1989. "Shinoyama Shikako no ichi shitai." In *Modan toshi bungaku II: Modan gāru no yūwaku*. Heibonsha.

Nagahara Hiroyuki. 2000. "Seisa to intonēshon no parametorikkusu." *Kotoba*, vol. 21, pp. 37–44.

Nagano Masaru. 1955. "Nihongo no kojinsa." In *Kōza Nihongo IV: Nihongo shujusō*. Ōtsuki shoten.

Nagasawa Mitsu. 1962. *Josei waka taikei*. Kazama shobō.

Nakajima Etsuko. 1993. "Kyōdō kenkyū, josei no kotoba to sedai II: Hanashikotoba ni arawareru sedai-sa: shukuyakukei." *Kotoba*, vol. 14, pp. 70–85.

———. 1994. "Josei no kotoba to bunmatsu no gengo keishiki." *Kotoba*, vol. 15, pp. 36–52.

———. 1996. "Kyōdō kenkyū: shokuba ni okeru josei no hanashikotoba, sono 4: Bunmatsu no gengo keishiki--gimon hyōgen ni okeru teineido no yōin." *Kotoba*, vol. 17, pp. 115–29.

Nakamura Momoko. 1995. *Kotoba to feminizumu*. Keisō shobō.

———. 2001. *Kotoba to jendā*. Keisō shobō.

Namura Jōhaku, ed. 1981. *Onna chōhōki* (Record of important matters for women). Bensiesha.

NHK Kotoba Chōsa Gurūpu, ed. 1980. *Nihonjin to hanashikotoba*. Nihon hosō shuppankai.

—NHK. 1980. "Gendaijin no hanashi kotoba." *Bunken geppō*. NHK.

—NHK. 1984. "Sedai to gengo ishiki." *Hōsō kenkyū to chōsa*. NHK, June.

—NHK. 1986. "Nihongo wa yahari midarete iru ka." *Hōsō kenkyū to chōsa*. NHK, July.

—NHK. 1986. "Hataraku josei no kotoba no ishiki." *Hōsō kenkyū to chōsa*. NHK, November.

—NHK. 1995. *Joshi kyōiku shi* (A history of women's education). NHK Radio, April 5, noted herein as *Joshi kyōiku shi*.

Nihon bunpō daijiten. Meiji shoin, 1971.

"Nihon no jogaku." *Fukkoku Nihon no fujin zasshi*, vol. 1. Ōzorasha, 1986.

Nishio Minoru. 1955. "Moji shiyō no rekishi." In *Gengo to seikatsu*, pp. 157–63. Mainichi shinbunsha.

Nomoto Kikuo. 1981. "Sei sabetsu to jisho." *Bungaku*, vol. 49, no. 10, pp. 94–102.

Nomura Masaaki. 1991. "Rakugo no josei to kotoba." *Kokubungaku kaishaku to kanshō*, vol. 56, no. 7, pp. 46–51.

Nonomura Kaizō. 1931. *Kyōgen shūsei*. Shun'yōdō.

Oda Michiko. 1999. "Keigo to bunmatsu hyōgen ni miru wakai josei no kotoba no hen'yō." *Kotoba*, vol. 20, pp. 191–94.

Ōhara Yumiko. 1993a. "Koe no takasa kara ukeru inshō ni tsuite." *Kotoba*, vol. 14, pp. 14–19.

_____. 1993b. "'Onna kotoba' no picchi." *Nihongogaku* (special extra issue for May), pp. 141–47.

_____. 2004. "Prosody and Gender in Workplace Interaction: Exploring Constraints and Resources in the Use of Japanese." In *Japanese Language, Gender, and Ideology: Cultural Models and Real People*, pp. 222–39. Edited by Okamoto Shigeko and Janet S. Shibamoto Smith. New York: Oxford University Press.

Ōishi Hatsutarō. 1980. "Seibetsu, nenreibetsu keigo shiyō." *Senshū kokubun*, vol. 26, pp. 17–40.

_____. 1996. "Joseigo no hensen." *Bunkyō daigaku kokubun*, vol. 25, pp. 1–9.

Okamoto Shigeko, and Janet S. Shibamoto Smith, eds. 2004. *Japanese Language, Gender, and Ideology: Cultural Models and Real People*. New York: Oxford University Press.

Ōkubo Tadatoshi. 1956a. "Josei to kotoba no utsukushisa." In *Kotobazukai no shinri*. Rokugatsusha.

_____. 1956b. "Onna kotoba 2." In *Machi no gengogaku*, pp. 9–10. Kawade shobō.

Om Chonmi. 1997. "Danjo-sa no hikaku: Omo ni teineisa (politeness) no kanten kara." *Kotoba*, vol. 18, pp. 27–40.

_____. 1999. "Teineisa ni okeru feminizumu gengo kenkyū no saikō." *Kotoba*, vol. 20, pp. 115_27.

Onna chōhoki hoka (Record of important matters for women and other texts). 1981. Edited by Kinsei bungaku shoshi kenkyūkai. Benseisha.

Ōshima Kaori. 1990. "Onna ga onna wo yakusu toki." *Hon'yaku no sekai*, vol. 9, no. 8, pp. 42–43.

Ozaki Kōyō shū. Kadokawa shoten, 1971.

Ozaki Yoshimitsu. 1994. "Shū joshi ni tsuite—datsu 'Josei sen'yōgo' shiyō no keikō." In *Shokuba ni okeru josei no hanashikotoba: Shizen danwa rokuon shiryō ni motozuite*, pp. 35–50. Tōkyō josei zaidan 1993 nen-do josei kenkyū hōkokusho.

_____. 1997. "Josei sen'yō bunmatsu keishiki no ima." In *Josei no kotoba: Shokuba hen*, pp. 33–58. Edited by Gendai Nihongo Kenkyūkai. Hitsuji shobō.

_____. 1988 (with Endō Orie). "Josei no kotoba no hensen: *koto, -te yo, da wa* wo chūshin ni." *Nihongogaku*, vol. 17, no. 5, pp. 56–79.

Peng, F.C. 1984. "Nihongo ni okeru seisa no hassei." *Hon'yaku no sekai*, vol. 9, no. 8, pp. 21–25.

Reinolds, Katsue Akiba, ed. 1993. *Onna to Nihongo*. Yūshindō.

_____. 2000. "Nihongo ni okeru seisa-ka: Ōbeigo to no hikaku taishō kara miete kuru mono." In *Joseigaku kyōiku no chōsen*, pp. 38–46. Edited by Watanabe Kazuko and Kanaya Chieko. Akashi shoten.

Saeki Ariyoshi. 1942. *Bushidō zensho*. Jidaisha.

Saeki Umetomo. 1936. *Kokugo shi: Jōko hen*. Tōkō shoin.

Sakuma Kanae. 1942. "Hyōjungo to joshi no kotobazukai." In *Nihongo no tame ni*. Kōseikaku.

Sakuma Mayumi. 1979. "Josei no ronri to bunshō." In *Josei to bunka, shakai, bosei, rekishi*, pp. 55–95. Hakuba shobō.

Sakurai Takashi. 2001. "'Sekuhara'—shokuba ni okeru kotoba no jyosei sabetsu." In *Onna to kotoba—onna wa kawatta ka nihongo wa kawatta ka*, pp. 153–61. Edited by Endō Orie. Akashi shoten.

Sasaki Eri. 1996. "Eigo no sei sabetsugo to Nihonjin e no eikyō: Eigo kyōkasho no chōsa to tomo ni." *Kotoba*, vol. 17, pp. 13–27.

_____. 1997. "Kyōkasho ni okeru bungaku to feminizumu: hyōgen wa jiyū de aru ka?" *Kotoba*, vol. 18, pp. 41–55.

_____. 1998. "Kyōkasho no naka no bungaku ni hyōgen sareru jendā baiasu: kōtō gakkō 'Eigo II' no bungaku wo yomu." *Kotoba*, vol. 19, pp. 106–27.

Sasaki Mizue. 1999. *Onna no Nihongo Otoko no Nihongo*. Chikuma shobō.

_____. 2000. *Onna to otoko no Nihongo jiten jō, ge*. Tōkyōdō shuppan.

_____, ed. 2006. *Nihongo to jendā*. Hitsuji shobō.

Satake Kuniko. 1984. "Jisho ni miru joseikan:Shōgakusei yōgo jiten no yōrei kara." *Gengo seikatsu* 387, pp. 62–68.

_____. 1995. "Onna no buntai, otoko no buntai: Shinbun tōsho wo shiryō ni." *Kotoba*, vol. 16, pp. 52–68.

_____. 1996a. "Onna to otoko no kakarekata: Taishū shōsetsu no sekkusu byōsha." *Kotoba*, vol. 17, pp. 73–84.

_____. 1998. "Onna kotoba, otoko kotoba: Kihan wo megutte." *Kotoba*, vol. 19, pp. 53–68.

_____. 1999. "Onna kotoba, otoko kotoba: Kihan wo megutte, shōgaku kokugo kyōkasho no baai." *Kotoba*, vol. 20, pp. 44–65.

_____. 2002. "Nihongo no jendā kihankeisei wo megutte—'Jogaku zasshi' no gensetsu." *Kotoba*, vol. 23, pp. 59–70.

_____. 2003. "Terebi anime no ruhusuru 'Onna kotoba/Otoko kotoba' kihan." *Kotoba*, vol. 24, pp. 43–59.

Seidensticker, Edward G., trans. 1976. *The Tale of Genji*. New York: Knopf.

Shibamoto, Janet. 1985. *Japanese Women's Language*. New York: Academic Press.

_____. 1992. "Women in Charge: Politeness and Directives in the Speech of Japanese Women." *Language in Society*, vol. 21, no. 1, pp. 59–82.

_____. 2002. "Kotoba ni yoru sekushuaritī no kōchiku." *Gengo, Tokushū: Gengo no jendā sutadīzu*, vol. 31, no. 2, pp. 68–69.

Shimada Isao. 1971a. "Kindaigo no goi II." In *Kōza Kokugoshi* 3, pp. 243–343. Edited by Sakakura Atsuyoshi and Ide Itaru. Taishūkan.

_____. 1971b. *Nyōbō kotoba to yūjo kotoba* (The language of the ladies-in-waiting and the language of prostitutes). In *Kōza kokugoshi goishi* (Japanese language history seminar, the history of vocabulary). Taishūkan shoten.

"Shinpen shūshin kyōten." Nihon kyōkasho taikei kindaihen 2 shūshin 2. Kōdansha, 1962.

Shioda Ryōhei. 1965. "Onna kotoba." In *Kokugo zuihitsu*. Sekkasha.

Shirayanagi Shūko. 1920. "Nihon bungaku ni arawareru fujin mondai." In *Nihon bungaku kōza^I*. Shinchōsha.

"Shōgaku sahō sho." Nihon Kyōkasho taikei kindaihen 2 shūshin 2. Kōdansha, 1962.

Sōgō Joseishi Kenkyūkai, ed. 1993. *Nihon josei no rekishi, bunka, shisō*. Kadokawa shoten.

Sōseki zenshū 1 (Works of Natsume Sōseki, vol. 1). Iwanami shoten, 1965.

Spender, Dale. 1980. *Man Made Language*. London and Boston: Routledge and Kegan Paul. Translated into Japanese by Katsue Akiba Reynolds as *Kotoba wa otoko ga shihaisuru*. Keisō shobō, 1987.

Sugimoto Tsutomu. 1967. "Nyōbō kotoba no keifu." In *Kindai Nihongo no shin kenkyū*. Ōfūsha.

_____. 1975. *Onna kotoba shi*. Yūzankaku.

_____. 1985a. *Edo no onna kotoba: asobase to arinsu to*. Sōtakusha.

_____. 1985b. *Onna no kotoba shi* (Documentations of women's language). Yūzankaku.

Sunaoshi Yukako. 2004. "Farm Women's Professional Discourse in Ibarki." In *Japanese Language, Gender, and Ideology: Cultural Models and Real People*, pp. 187–204. Edited by Okamoto Shigeko and Janet S. Shibamoto Smith. New York: Oxford University Press.

Suzuki Bunshirō. 1948. "Nihongo no kaikyūsei to seibetsusei." In *Bunshirō zuihitsu*. Chūō kōronsha.

Suzuki Chizu. 1998. "'Joseigo' wo tayō suru dansei wa 'okama' ka?" *Kotoba*, vol. 19, pp. 69–91.

_____. 1999. "Bunmatsu hyōgen no intonēshon no danjosa." *Kotoba*, vol. 20, pp. 75–82.

Suzuki Kazue. 1992. "Masu media no naka no josei." *Kotoba*, vol. 13, pp. 28–31.

Tabata Yasuko. 1996. *Nyonin seiji no chūsei: Hōjō Masako to Hino Tomiko*. Kōdansha.

Takasaki Midori. 1988. "Mosakuki no joseigo." *Kotoba*, vol. 9, pp. 23–40.

_____. 1992. "Joseigo to Nihongogaku: Josei kotoba no shisō no moderu." *Kotoba*, vol. 13, pp. 46–51.

_____. 1993. "Josei no kotoba to kaisō." *Nihongogaku* (special extra issue for May), pp. 169–80.

_____. 1994. "Teian: Kotoba kara hiku Nihon no josei no 'ima' jiten." *Kotoba*, vol. 15, pp. 28–35.

_____. 1996. "Terebi to joseigo." *Nihongogaku*, vol. 15, no. 10, pp. 46–56.

_____. 1997. "Josei no hatarakikata to kotoba no tayōsei." In *Josei no kotoba: Shokuba hen*, pp. 213–39. Edited by Gendai Nihongo Kenkyūkai. Hitsuji shobō.

_____. 2002. "Dansei no hatarakikata to kotoba no tayōsei." In *Dansei no kotoba: Shokuba hen*, pp. 207–35. Hitsuji shobō.

Tamamura Fumio, ed. 1995. *Nihongogaku wo manabu hito no tame ni* (For students of Japanese language studies). Sekaishisōsha.

Tanaka Akio. 1978. "Goi no isōsa." In *Kokugo goiron*, pp. 212–48. Meiji shoin.

Tanaka Katsuyoshi, ed. 1987. *Kyōikushi*. Kawashima shoten.

Tanaka Kazuko. 1990a. "Shinbun shimen ni arawareta jendā." *Kokugakuin hōgaku*, vol. 28, no. 1, pp. 87–119.

_____. 1990b. "Shinbun kateimen no joseigaku." *Kokugakuin hōgaku*, vol. 28, no. 2, pp. 1–49.

Tanaka Sumie. 1964. "Otoko kotoba to onna kotoba." In *Hōsō bunka*. Nihon hōsō kyōkai.

Tanaka Sumiko. 1956. "Josei no danseika to onnarashisa." *Fujin kōron* (February), pp. 78–83.

Tannen, Deborah. 1990. *You Just Don't Understand: Women and Men in Conversation*. New York: William Morrow. Translated into Japanese by Tamaru Misuzu as *Wakariaeru riyū, wakariaenai riyū*. Kōdansha, 2003.

Toki Zenmaro. 1957. "Wakai josei no kotoba." In *Kokugo zuihitsu*, pp. 49–56. Sekkasha.

Tōkyō Josei Zaidan, ed. 1998. *"Kotoba" ni miru josei*. Kureyon hausu.

Tokutomi Roka, Kinoshita Naoe, Iwano Hōmei shū. Gendai bungaku taikei 16. Chikuma shobō, 1966.

"Tsubouchi Shōyō shū." Meiji bungaku zenshū, vol. 16. Chikuma shobō, 1966.

Tsukamoto Tetsuzō, ed. 1928. *Jokai*. In *Onna shiso* (The four books for women). Yūhōdō.

Tsukishima Yutaka. 1972. "Kodai no moji." In *Kōza kokugo shi*, vol. 2, pp. 311–444. Taishūkan shoten.

Ueno Chizuko, ed. 1996. *Kitto kaerareru josei sabetsugo: Watashitachi no gaidorain*. Sanseidō.

Uno Yoshikata. 1986. *Gengo seikatsu shi*. Tōkyōdō shuppan.

_____. 1971. "Otoko kotoba , onna kotoba." *Kokubungaku kaishaku to kyōzai no kenkyū*. Gakutōsha, January.

Usami Mayumi. 1997. *Kotoba wa shakai wo kaerareru*. Akashi shoten.

Wakita Haruko, ed. 1987. *Nihon josei shi*. Yoshikawa kōbunkan.

_____, et al., ed. 1992. *Nihon josei shi*. Yoshikawa kōbunkan.

_____. 1995. *Chūsei ni ikiru onnatachi* (Iwanami shinsho). Iwanami shoten.

Waley, Arthur, trans. 1957–58. *The Tale of Genji*. New York: Allen and Unwin.

Washi Rumi. 2004. "'Japanese Female Speech' and Language Policy in the World War II Era." In *Japanese Language, Gender, and Ideology: Cultural Models and Real People*, pp. 76–91. Edited by Okamoto Shigeko and Janet S. Shibamoto Smith. New York: Oxford University Press.

Watanabe Tomosuke. 1991. "Sabetsugo to josei." *Kokubungaku kaishaku to kanshō*, vol. 56, no. 7, pp. 52–58.

Wo Mison. 1981. "Jisho ni miru josei: kokugo jiten kyōdō kenkyū, danseigo to joseigo." *Kotoba*, vol. 2, pp. 50–57.

Yabe Hiroko. 1995 (with Endō Orie). "Kyōdō kenkyū: Shokuba ni okeru josei no hanashikotoba, sono 3: Hanashikotoba ni tokuchōteki na go no atarashii yōhō to sedai-sa." *Kotoba*, vol. 16, pp. 114–27.

_____. 1996. "Shinbun hōdō no gaikokujin danwa ni miru danjosa: buntai to kaku joshi shiyō no kankei wo chūshin ni." *Kotoba*, vol. 17, pp. 58–72.

_____. 2001. "Orinpikku hōdō ni egakareru joseitachi." In *Onna to kotoba— onna wa kawatta ka Nihongo wa kawatta ka*, pp. 171–79. Edited by Endō Orie. Akashi shoten.

Yamakawa Kikue. 1956. *Onna nidai no ki* (Records of two generations of women). Nihon hyōron shinsha.

Yamazaki Hisayuki. 1963. *Kokugo taigū hyōgen taikei no kenkyū: kinsei hen*. Musashino Shoin.

Yanagi Yae. 1941. "*Fujin no kotoba*." *Kokugo bunka kōza dai 5 kan nihongo seikatsu hen*. Asahi Shinbunsha.

Yasuhara Teishitsu. 1978. *Katakoto* (Faltering words). Edited by Shiraki Susumu. Kasama sensho.

Yazaki Genkurō. 1960. *Kore kara no Nihongo*. Mikasa shobō.

Yomiuri shinbun. April 20, 1995.

Yoneda Masato. 1986. "Fūfu no yobikata: ankēto chōsa no kekka kara." *Gengo seikatsu* 416, pp. 18–21.

Yonekawa Akihiko. 1994. "Wakai josei no kotoba no shinriteki, shakaiteki haikei." *Nihongogaku*, vol. 13, no. 10, pp. 4–18.

_____. 1995. *Joshi daisei kara mita rōjingo jiten*. Bunrikaku.

_____. 1997a. *Gendai wakamono kotoba kō*. Maruzen kabushiki kaisha.

_____. 1997b. *Wakamono kotoba jiten*. Tōkyōdō shuppan.

Yoshida Ken'ichi. 1955. "*Nihon wa dore dake amerikanaizu sarertaka*." In *Fujin kōron*. Chūō kōronsha.

Yoshida Sumio. 1935. "Fujin no kotoba." In *Kotoba no kōza dai ni shō*. Nihon hōsō shuppan kyōkai.

_____. 1952a. "Fujin no kotoba." In *Kinseigo to kinsei bungaku* (Modern literature and the modern lexicon), pp. 33–40. Tōyōkan shuppansha.

_____. 1952b. "'Naniwa dora' yōgo kō." In *Kinsei to kinsei bungaku* (Modern literature and the modern lexicon), pp. 41–53. Tōyōkan shuppansha.

Yoshimoto Banana. 1988. *Kicchin.* Fukutake shoten.

Yoshioka Yasuo. 1994. "Wakai josei no gengo kōdō." *Nihongogaku,* vol. 13, no. 10, pp. 33–44.

Yoshizawa Yoshinori. 1934. "Hiragana no kenkyū." In *Kokugo kagaku kōza VIII: Mojigaku,* pp. 3–44. Meiji shoin.

Yūhōdō Bunko, ed. 1911. *Ekiken jikkun jō* (Ekiken's ten doctrines for women). Yūhōdō.

Yuzawa Kōkichirō. 1964. *Kuruwa kotoba no kenkyū.* Meiji shoin.

INDEX

women tutors, 21
work outside the home, 82, 83, 88
workplace language, 92–95, 99
wotoko, 5
wotome, 5

Y
yaku, 100
Yamada Waka, 71
Yamanoe no Okura, 6–7
Yamato Court, 20
Yamato kotoba, 47, 49, 53
Yamoto nadeshiko, 77, 83
Yanagida Kunio, 74n2
Yanagi Yae, 77, 100
yara, 98n3
yarite, 52
Yashinaigusa (Fujin yashingaigusa), 46–48
Yasuhara Teishitsu, 45–46

Yazaki Genkurō, 85–86
yin and yang, 62
yo, 2, 30
Yokoi Tokio, 65
yokutte yo, 63, 64
Yomiuri Shinbun (newspaper), 97
Yonekawa Akihiko, 101–2, 109–10
Yo no fujo tachi ni susumu (Council for
    Women of the World), 58
Yoshida Kenkō, 25, 85
Yoshida Sumio, 35
Yoshimoto Banana, 95–96
Yoshizawa Yoshinori, 14, 16
Yue Fū, 14
yūjogo, 2, 3

Z
zaamasu, 83
zomeku, 52

ABOUT THE AUTHOR

Endō Orie is a professor in the Department of Cultural Linguistics at the Ko-shigaya Campus of Bunkyō University (Tokyo) with a teaching specialization in social linguistics and Japanese language pedagogy. Her best-known works are *Ki ni naru kotoba: Nihongo no saikentō* (Words That Concern Me: A Reconsideration of the Japanese Language) (Nanundō, 1987); *Onna no kotoba no bunka-shi* (Gakuyō shobō, 1997), the book on which *A Cultural History of Japanese Women's Language* is based; and *Chūgoku onna moji kenkyū* (A Study of Chinese Women's Script) (Meiji shoin, 2002). She is also co-author of *Sen-jichū no hanashi kotoba: rajio dorama daihon kara* (Spoken Japanese during War-time: Radio Drama) (Hitsuji shobō, 2004). Professor Endō's recent research projects include a historical study of a Chinese women's script referred to as "Nushu" from Hunan Province and a project that draws on radio drama scripts and family magazines as a source for examining Japanese language usage during the Asian Pacific War, and its legacy for contemporary speakers of Japanese.